BE LIKE A TREE

Be Like a Tree

Zen Talks by Thích Phước Tịnh

Edited and Illustrated
by
Karen Hilsberg

O

Jasmine Roots Press
2008

Published by
Jasmine Roots Press

Printed by
www.lulu.com

Paperback
Library of Congress Cataloging in Publication Data

Hilsberg, Karen.
Be Like a Tree: Zen Talks by Thích Phước Tịnh
1. Mindfulness   2. Zen Buddhism
3. Meditation   4. Thích Phước Tịnh
5. Thích Nhất Hạnh

ISBN- 978-0-615-25028-1

Waking up this morning, I smile
Twenty-four brand new hours are before me.
I vow to look on all beings
With the eyes of love and compassion.

Thích Nhất Hạnh

You know, a tree is always there for you.
If you are open, you can see the whole tree.

Rabbi Don Ani Shalom Singer

Life, death, peace, and joy
Are coming together beautifully.
Human relationships are nice in so many ways.
A moment you come,
A moment of love and care
Turning everything into eternal light.

Thầy Giác Thanh

To my ancestors,
my parents Sol and Diane Rosenthal,
my siblings Rob Rosenthal,
Pam and Dave Reynolds,
my husband Bruce Hilsberg,
my children Emily and Ben Hilsberg,
and my descendants,
who are all supporting me
on the path

CONTENTS

PREFACE

Traditionally, the practice of mindfulness has been taught in the context of a personal, long-term relationship between teacher and student, master and disciple. Most often, these relationships took place between and among monastics, although since the time of the Buddha over 2,500 years ago, the teachings were also made available to lay practitioners (also known as householders) such as Anathapindika. In this life, I have had the great good fortune to receive the teachings of such a teacher, the Venerable Thích Phước Tịnh, referred to often as "the Venerable."

After spending most of his life in Vietnam, where he ordained as a monk as a young man, and where he became the abbot of a beautiful temple in Dalat, he came to live in Southern California. After spending his life in Vietnam and offering teachings to monastics and lay practitioners, he came to the West and began offering teachings in Vietnamese to monastic and lay practitioners in San Diego County, Orange County, Los Angeles County, and at Deer Park Monastery in Escondido where he currently resides. All of his talks are presented in his native tongue, and some are simultaneously translated into English. I remember the first dharma talks I attended in the small meditation hall in Solidity Hamlet in the summer and fall of 2003. I was impressed that the Venerable was such a masterful storyteller who could assemble a talk like a quilter assembles a quilt, laying all the patches down carefully and then sewing them together to make a whole that is much greater than the sum of its parts.

As a labor of love, I have transcribed some of his talks by hand during the simultaneous translations and edited them into book form in order to share the dharma with English-speaking practitioners.

The Venerable and I came to know one another personally during a time of great crisis in my life, when my husband of fifteen years was dying of pancreatic cancer. The Venerable wrote us two very inspirational letters to help us through our difficulties. This is one of them:

> *We, the Easterners or Westerners, young or old, we are always very fearful when we are facing death. From the day that we are healthy to the moment that we are ill and our breath is irregular, we still don't believe that we are facing death. Of course this physical body is disintegrating but we still don't accept that. And that belief is deep in our consciousness. But there is an ultimate truth, and this is based on how deep our awareness is and how strongly you believe in your own self. Life is a cycle of manifestation, and death is a cycle of de-manifestation. But we are the awareness that is no-birth no-death.*
>
> *Just like the trees in the winter time, the leaves fall and the branches are bare. But we cannot say that during that three-month period the tree is dead, because the living energy still exists. We know that in springtime the young shoots and new leaves will return fresh and develop very fast. Our human life is a miracle, and is a thousand*

times more miraculous than the trees during the changing.

If the tree uses the cycle of rest so that it can grow, human beings should look at the life and death of this physical body just like a cycle so that they can mature in the spiritual life. This is the reason that when you look deeply into your own mind you won't have any worry, fear or despair.

And I myself am not a good practitioner, and I have many sufferings when I see that my loved ones are very sick and I cannot help them, and I have to face many of my friends leaving, and I do not have the power to hold them back.

But because of the practice eventually I can transform my fear and suffering in my heart. I have strong faith that our True Self is no-birth no-death, and life and death of this physical body is only a period of the manifestation and de-manifestation of this no-birth no-death of our True Self.

Bodhisattvas or Zen masters, they come to this world and they leave this world very peacefully and freely. They can say goodbye to this life with joy because they surely know that we are not forever gone. We are no different than these bodhisattvas or Zen masters. We need a strong belief in one thing, that this physical body is having illness and having pain and it is here and

then gone, but our life, our True Self, or the
awareness is never gone.

I sincerely hope that you have strong faith in
your Buddha nature that is no-birth no-
death, that is your True Self, so you can
overcome despair, worry, sadness and
suffering. And I pray that the Three Jewels
of the Ten Directions will always protect
you so that you will have strong faith in
yourself.

Venerable Thích Phước Tịnh
(Translated from Vietnamese text by Vân
Khánh Hà)

It is quite unusual for a Vietnamese monastic to
visit the home of a Western lay practitioner.
However, due the severity of my husband's illness
and the conditions being favorable, the Venerable
compassionately accepted an invitation to visit our
home in the spring of 2005. My husband was not
well during the visit, and so the Venerable
proceeded to offer guidance to me that proved
extremely helpful in the ensuing weeks and months.
He encouraged me to determine what kind of help I
needed, to evaluate who could successfully provide
that help, and to ask for and graciously accept the
help offered. He watered my wholesome seeds,
praised the resilience of women, and encouraged me
to "Be like a tree," which became a koan for me. He
urged me to stay firmly rooted, even as the storm of
my husband's illness tossed around my branches
and leaves. Over the years, I have pondered the
question, "What does it mean to be like a tree?"
After my husband's death, I was inspired to return

to painting, a passion from my earlier life, and I painted a number of trees as I explored this question in the context of my mindfulness practice. These paintings are included as illustrations in this book.

Two weeks before my husband's death, my husband and I went to Deer Park Monastery and shared tea with the Venerable after his dharma talk (*Life, Death, and Karma*). I clearly remember the joy I felt listening to this wise Zen master as he encouraged my husband not to fight death but instead to make peace with himself and those around him.

This truth helped my husband and our family enormously, and I thought to myself, "How can I experience such happiness and freedom when my husband is dying?" I have come to believe that the answer is this: through clearly seeing reality as it was in that moment (i.e. that my husband was dying), rather than seeing it as I wanted it to be (i.e. that I wished my husband would not die), I felt the relief and bliss of the truth of the situation. And my understandings continue to grow as I am able to look at life and accept it (in the words of Fr. Thomas Keating) "just as it is in this moment without having to know all the details or trying to manipulate it." That was a healing moment for me and continues to inform my way of living.

What it means to me now to be like a tree is to be myself, to be grounded, to bend with the weather but not to break, and to be a home and safe haven for others. Be like a tree also means to seek refuge: in nature, in the earth, the sun, the air, the rain and in reality as it is. Trees detoxify the air by taking in carbon dioxide and releasing oxygen for us to breathe. Trees have become my friends and teachers.

There are several appendices after the Zen talks. Appendix One is a biographical essay written by the Venerable after the passing of his dear friend Thầy Giác Thanh, the first abbot of Deer Park Monastery. Following his friend's death, the Venerable was asked by our teacher Thích Nhất Hạnh to reside at Deer Park Monastery as the spiritual elder of the community. Appendix Two is a letter that was sent in a package of letters from our friends at Deer Park Monastery during the time of my husband's illness. Appendix Three is an interview with the Venerable previously published in the Deer Park Breeze, a newsletter for the community. Appendix Four and Five are summaries of informal conversations between a small of students and the Venerable while enjoying Oolong tea in the room where he receives visitors at Deer Park Monastery.

I have been lucky to receive these life-changing teachings. I am grateful to the Venerable for his presence here in Southern California. For many years, his teachings have been available to the Vietnamese community in the form of compact discs, and a book of his teachings has been published in Vietnamese this year on the Forty-Two Chapters Sutra. The Venerable has dreamed of a book of talks in English, and it is my heartfelt aspiration to bring the Venerable's beautiful teachings to English-speaking practitioners like myself. I transcribed these talks by hand as they were simultaneously translated from Vietnamese to English at Deer Park Monastery during Days of

Mindfulness and retreats. I learned from my bilingual friends that the poetic nature of the Venerable's talks is frequently lost in translation. I regret that even more may have been lost in my single-handed efforts to transcribe, interpret, and edit these talks. The Venerable asked me not to translate these talks verbatim, but rather to incorporate them into my life. From that perspective, he requested that I share my understanding of the dharma with my English-speaking friends.

I have done my best to be true to the intention of the teachings and to present them in a readable format based on my ever evolving understandings of the practice and the dharma. I accept full responsibility for the errors, lapses, inaccuracies and inconsistencies in the text.

Regarding the text itself, each chapter begins with a quotation from that talk which highlights the theme of the talk. Words in brackets indicate that they have been added for the purpose of clarification. My wish is that in spite of this highly imperfect process, the dharma will be clear and these teachings will help the reader to discover peace and reality as it is.

Karen Hilsberg
November 6, 2008

ACKNOWLEDGEMENTS

There are many people who have contributed to the manifestation of this book, whether they know it or not. I thank you all. I offer my heartfelt gratitude to the Venerable Thích Phước Tịnh for envisioning this book in English, for entrusting these teachings to me and for encouraging me in this project for the past four years.

These teachings have all been offered to the community of practice at Deer Park Monastery in Escondido, California in Vietnamese. The talks were simultaneously translated by a number of spiritual friends without whom this book would not have been possible. Thanks to Thầy Pháp Hỷ, Thầy Pháp Khôi, Thầy Pháp Uyển, Thầy Pháp Hữu, Sư Cô Quy Nghiêm, Sư Cô Đẳng Nghiêm, Sư Cô Lăng Nghiêm, Sư Cô Hành Nghiêm, Sư Cô Nho Nghiêm, Vân Khánh Hà, Mỹ Lê Nguyễn, and Natalie Trần. I bow in gratitude to you for sharing the dharma by simultaneously translating these talks and other conversations with the Venerable into English.

Special thanks to Most Venerable Thích Nhất Hạnh and Sư Cô Chân Không for introducing me to the practice of mindfulness in 1993 at a Day of Mindfulness in Malibu, California, for transmitting the Five Mindfulness Trainings to me, for being my teachers, for founding Deer Park Monastery in Southern California, and for supporting my ordination into the Order of Interbeing.

I am very grateful to my friends and mentors Thầy Pháp Trí and Denise Nguyễn who have generously offered me and my family instruction in the art of mindfulness and sangha-building from 2003 to the present. Thanks to Peggy Rowe Ward and Larry Ward for believing in me and for sharing so much wisdom and laughter. My gratitude goes to Marilyn and Dale Withers for their feedback on an early draft of this book and to Michael Nguyễn and my friend Beatrice for editorial suggestions that made the book more readable in English. Thanks to Sara Jenkins who encouraged me to forge ahead when I contemplated giving up on this project.

I so appreciate Germaine Franco, Sarah Albright, Douglas Dick, Corine Whitman, Aubyn Stahmer, Carl Stahmer, Rebekah Henty, Tom Drake and Thầy Pháp Hải for being such loyal, wonderful and inspirational friends to me. Thanks to Nancy Miller and Melanie Lenington for their emotional support, and to Bruce Anderson and Alisa Rosseter for encouraging me to paint again. Thanks to Shari Friedrichsen for supporting my yoga practice, to my colleagues at the Department of Mental Health who support my daily mindfulness practice in my workplace, and to my children for patiently witnessing my work on "the book." And my gratitude goes to my many friends on the path at Deer Park Monastery, in the Ripening Sangha, in Organic Garden Sangha, and in Jasmine Roots Sangha. I am blessed to know you in this lifetime.

Last but not least, thanks to Alex Cline for copy editing this book and for continuing to encourage me in this project until it has come to fruition. Thanks to David Viafora for being a sounding board and for encouragement during the past year, to Carolyn Marsden and Kenley Neufeld for

encouraging me to self-publish this book through
www.lulu.com, to Jordan Whitman for designing
the beautiful cover and for creative guidance, and to
Vivian Alvarez and Sol Rosenthal for masterfully
proofreading and editing the final manuscript. This
book would not have come into being without the
constant friendship, guidance and patience of Vân
Khánh Hà who introduced me to the Venerable and
has supported this book in every way, shape, and
form from the beginning to its completion. You are
all true spiritual friends to me and my family.

Fifty percent of the profits from sales of this book
will be donated to the Touching and Helping
Program of the Unified Buddhist Church which
helps many people in Vietnam to improve their
living conditions, to feel the love of humanity and
to pursue a higher spiritual path by providing day
care and preschools to poor families in the
countryside. The other fifty percent of the profits
from sales of this book will be donated to service
projects supported by the Quan Âm Temple in Đa
Lạt, Việt Nam.

DHARMA TALKS

CHAPTER ONE
Is There Any Dharma Door?

*There is a whispering voice inside our heads
providing a running commentary on our lives. The
whispering voice identifies with all the emotions.
We can get lost in the ocean of suffering if we
believe in the whispering voice. Instead of listening
to the whispering voice, stand on the shore and just
watch all those emotions come and go, like waves
ebbing and flowing on the sand.*

Praise to Shakyamuni Buddha, the Fully
Enlightened One.

The *practice* of mindfulness is very important in the
Southern or Mahayana tradition. The teachings of
the Buddha are all about the practice, not about
knowledge. In the Southern Tradition, we practice
with each movement of our body, and the stream of
practice has gone on like this for over a thousand
years.

In order to practice correctly, the most important
practice is to look into our own true mind. This
direct experience of oneself is a teaching of the
Buddha that transcends time, and we can experience
it for ourselves. This practice consists of skillfully
coming back to ourselves and dwelling in the
dharma, dwelling right in our bodies, dwelling right
in our thinking, dwelling right in our feelings,
dwelling right in our minds. Then we can see each
movement of our mind, and that is truly dwelling in
mindfulness. Next we can cut off afflictions, and
then we can experience joy and nirvana in this life.

If we do not do this, we are just floating through this life and can't realize anything.

I would like to introduce a Buddhist sutra in the Southern tradition that comes under the heading of "miscellaneous." These talks are still in their original form since they are not noticed or translated very often. They may not be the most polished or best sutras but they contain deep and profound teachings of the Buddha. The one I would like to share today is the Sutra Samutra Nikaya which can be translated into English as, "Is There Any Dharma Door?"

The text of the sutra goes like this. Buddha asked, "Bhikkhus, is there any dharma door that doesn't need faith, forbearance, rationalization, or deep listening and that can still bring us to the true teaching and experience of nirvana in this life?" The Bhikkhus replied, "World Honored One, please teach us."

The Buddha taught: "There is a dharma door in which you do not need faith, listening, thinking, or forbearance, and that dharma practice can help you to transcend all afflictions. When your eye is in contact with a form, you recognize it as it is. If you hear something, you recognize it as it is. If your nose gives rise to craving or aversion, just recognize it. This process can help you to transcend afflictions and to realize nirvana in this life."

This teaching can bring you tremendous peace and joy. To take this a step further, when you feel sad, be aware of your sadness. When you are grasping, be aware of your grasping. And so on. I believe that the practice recommended by this sutra surpasses the benefits of all the one thousand and seven dharma koans studied by many Buddhists. All you need to do is dwell in the awareness of your mental state, and then you can touch nirvana.

Why do we bring the mind back to the body so it can dwell in the body? Because we have a habit energy in which the mind is never dwelling in the body. The mind goes ahead of the body and leaves the body as if it were an empty house. Happiness is there when the mind and body are one. When we allow the mind to dwell in the body, then we find that we can heal our bodies. For example, in the olden days, people lived in the mountains and did not have access to and could not rely on medical interventions and doctors. Instead, they used this practice of bringing the mind to dwell in the breath and in the body in order to take care of and heal their organs and tissues.

We can speak to ourselves in a way that can inspire us, so that life can flow forth from our bodies. If people feel sick and uneasy, then sooner or later their bodies can become sick. There are some people who love life and can go through illness and yet still dwell peacefully in this life. Our consciousness affects how our illnesses progress. Let us speak to the cells in our bodies so our bodies can heal themselves.

When we walk, when we stand, when we wink or raise an eyebrow, if we shine the light of mindfulness on our bodies, then we are the masters of our bodies and can heal ourselves on a subtle level. Yoga practitioners can follow their breathing or hold their breath for 10-15 minutes. It seems very mysterious to us, but when the mind is calm and the breath is gentle and calm, then we can be in control of even the breath. This is how people who know that they are close to dying can control the time of their own death. When they feel as though their bodies are like a kerosene lamp that is running out of oil, they just hold their breath and then they die. They can go very gently. And when you can be the master of your own territory, this technique is not such a big secret. That's how they die. They just hold their breath because they are so close to the end, and the light goes out, and then they enter nirvana just like that. If you can become a better practitioner, you may be able to be in control of your own dying.

Dwelling in mindfulness of the body, you do not let your body go very far away. If there's a minute when the mind wanders somewhere else, just invite the master back to the house to bring the warmth of mindfulness to shine in. The old Zen masters [like Master Lin Chi] used stronger language like, "Without mindfulness, you are living your life like a corpse."

Let us try for a few days to practice the miracle of mindfulness in this way: let us concentrate on taking five to ten steps in mindfulness each day. Let us say to ourselves, "If I wasn't mindful before, then now, with each step I take, my mind will dwell in my body." This is a very simple practice. I use this practice in the following way. When I walk from my room down the hill to the dining hall, I require myself to be mindful of each of the fifty-seven steps on the staircase as I descend. If I am not mindful of each step, then I start over again, and I keep doing this until I can walk those steps in mindfulness. I do not eat my meal until I have walked all fifty-seven steps in mindfulness. When we can do this, naturally we become more in touch with our feelings. There's no way to be in control of our feelings if we can't first be in control of our body. Controlling our feelings is far more difficult than controlling our bodies. But the practice is the same. We simply recognize our feelings. When we are sad, we become aware of the sadness. When we are joyful, we become aware of the joyfulness. When we are worried, we become aware of the worries.

We recognize and become aware of our feelings of sadness, of joy, of worries, and of concerns. We recognize that these are feelings, but the feelings are not us. They are there; they manifest because there are conditions that cause them to manifest. The emotions and mental formations need nourishment to grow; they arise and grow because conditions are sufficient for them to manifest in that moment. If we don't continue to feed them with these conditions, they cannot survive. If we don't nourish them, they wither. Therefore our practice consists of two steps:

1) Do not feed the negative feelings and mental formations when they come up.
2) Nurture and nourish the positive feelings and mental formations when they come up.

For example, when the mind gives rise to irritation, anger, or negative emotions about a particular person, we must remember that these feelings can destroy our lives. Instead, look at the positive and lovely things about this particular person in order to nourish joy and happiness in our own minds. Remember, feelings come and go. Always dwell in mindfulness. Another way to say this is "No-birth and no-death," because mindfulness is always present.

There is a whispering voice inside our heads providing a running commentary on our lives. The whispering voice identifies with all the emotions. We can get lost in the ocean of suffering if we believe in the whispering voice. Instead of listening to the whispering voice, stand on the shore and just watch all those emotions come and go, like waves ebbing and flowing on the sand.

Someone once asked me, "When is the time when a husband and wife need each other the most?" My answer is this: the time when a husband and wife need each other most is when they are at their most difficult, heaviest, and most unlovely. When we are lovely, everyone loves us. We don't realize that we need our husband or our wife then. But when we are most unlovely, that is when we need our husband or wife the most.

Here's a little story. There is a woodsman who comes home every night and touches and rubs the leaves of a tree outside the house before he goes inside. When asked by a neighbor why he does that, touching the leaves before he enters the house, he gave this answer. Each night when he returns from cutting wood, he rubs the leaves of the tree and places all his worries and anxieties on the branch of the tree in the evening. Then he enters his home to spend time with his family. In the morning, when he goes back to work the next day, he picks his worries up again. But the next day, they seem lighter. Whatever he was so worried about in the evening, it lessens each day. This is so with us too. We can let go of our worries because our worries are not us.

In conclusion, be aware of the body and of every movement of the body. We forget and keep identifying ourselves with our sadness or joyful feelings, and then our lives just float away. Practice inviting the energy of mindfulness to shine light on everything, including your body and your feelings. Then we will realize the peace that already exists within our own souls.

CHAPTER TWO
Successful Parenting I

*What is the most important thing in life? To love
and be loved has always been a basic human desire.
We can do this by making a place for our children
in our hearts.*

*Let us aspire to cultivate our happiness. Why would
we want to drown ourselves in our worries,
calculations, sadness, fame, or position, when in
fact happiness is right here, right in front of our
eyes?*

Praise to Shakyamuni Buddha, the Fully Awakened
One.

Taking care of adults is much easier than taking
care of young people. Usually, older people come to
my talks. There are not a lot of young people who
come to my talks. What helps us to have a
connection with young people, to establish
communication with them, and to win them over?
The answer is this: Have an innocent mind, a mind
that is open. We need to cultivate our own
innocence and purity in ourselves in order to be able
to connect with a child. The second element we
need to cultivate is our own freshness. We have to
have a lot of freshness to have a connection with a
young person.

Children tend to be closer to their mothers than to
their fathers. Mothers often are not the
disciplinarians or the strict ones in the family.
Fathers more often like to appear stern, firm, and

disciplined because these are qualities that are needed in life. But at a younger age, children really need tenderness and care and a real connection with another. In order to be the person who can offer that connection to a child, we need to cultivate freshness and innocence in ourselves. This is of the utmost importance, because the greatest and most precious contribution we can make to society is to raise our children properly.

To contribute a caring, loving, properly raised child is our greatest contribution to society. We can do this by teaching our children the qualities of true beauty and happiness. A lay person asked the Dalai Lama, "How can I teach my child to have an ethical lifestyle and to know how to treasure pleasant qualities in life?" The Dalai Lama answered, "*You* must become a person who is truly beautiful and peaceful." Children don't need you to teach them. They learn from the way you live, and the way to really teach them is by modeling for them by the way *we* live our lives.

What is the most important thing in life? To love and be loved has always been a basic human desire. We can do this by making a place for our children in our hearts. Of course we need to eat and drink— but even more important is breathing. The air we breathe is more important than food and drink. We aren't living the life of a human being without breath and compassion. These are the foundations of a happy life and a healthy society.

Or we can look at this from the other way around. Our life is a waste if we have no one to love and if no one loves us. Human beings can endure many things, but a person cannot survive when he or she is lonely. Loneliness can seem like an abstract feeling, but it can create real suffering for human beings.

We really suffer when we lose the feeling of connection with our loved ones, whether this is between spouses or between parents and children. We need to fill our hearts with love as practitioners. Then, from this foundation we can stand on our own two feet as human beings and develop compassion. Then our lives become worthwhile. All the bad things that happen in the world begin with people who are lonely and without love in their lives.

Most of us here are parents, and we have experience with how to raise children and how to create love and happiness in our families. So let us ponder these topics:

1) Loving and returning love.
2) Love as a gift.

First, let us look into our own family lives, and from there we can look into the life of our society. Life in the family is the seed from which society grows. For example, a person who grows up with a lot of misfortunes and wounds beginning in childhood carries those wounds with him as he grows up. On the other hand, if there is happiness in the family, then the child will have a happy life. The greatest gift to society is the raising of happy, peaceful people. People with a lot of misfortunes spread a lot of misfortunes. However, if we put happiness, joy, and peace in our children's consciousness, then they continue to spread happiness, joy, and peace in society. But if we put a lot of sadness and suffering into their consciousness, they pour it out and recreate suffering in subsequent generations. Whatever we create in our families, that is what our society will become.

In our communities, the gap continues to get bigger between ourselves and our children. We are the ones who need to make that gap smaller and re-establish a connection so that we don't lose our children. There are not a lot of younger people at the temples to carry on the Buddhist traditions, for example. One reason is because the old teachers use old language which the young people cannot understand. So language could be one problem. Another problem is that the older people in the temples are not open to the younger generation. The young people in turn do not feel welcome and do not want to go there. If each temple would vow to ordain three young monks or nuns per year, then that would bring in the younger generation to the temples.

Similarly, we tend to reinforce this generation gap as parents. The way we think is old-fashioned. For example, in Asian culture, Taoism is deeply ingrained in our thinking. The nature of Taoism is very authoritative, especially from fathers to children, and that creates hierarchy. If we want to establish communication with our children, our hearts and minds should be open so that we can be on the same wavelength as our children. If we put great emphasis on form and authority, then we are the ones who are creating that gap. Then it is no wonder that our children want to go to college as soon as possible to get out of what they experience as the suffocating family situation. Then it is too late to correct our mistakes, the mistakes of the language gap and the generation gap created by our own thinking.

And yet in our family life, there is no greater suffering than the suffering of not being able to communicate with our loved ones. Not being able to communicate creates so much suffering! If there is something that is wrong or happening between ourselves and our loved ones, we need to take it on and re-establish communication as soon as possible. If you let these problems linger, they will damage your relationships. We can often resolve a lot of issues in our family lives if we do only one thing: establish communication. We must vow to develop our compassion so that we can be on the same wavelength as our children. They need our freshness and liveliness, and we need to rediscover our own pure spirit of innocence.

You might not agree with me. You may think, "I love my children, but they don't like me." You may believe that you are sacrificing a lot. You work so hard to create financial security so that you can meet their material needs, and then all they return to you is coldness, turning their backs on you. You feel you have put in a huge investment and are not getting what you expected in return. But sometimes the type of love we think the other person needs can become a prison for them. A gift may bring a lot of happiness, but a gift can also bring a lot of suffering if it is not what another person needs.

The second point to keep in mind is that we all have a deep need to be accepted in the human family.

Here's a funny science fiction story: On a distant planet the creatures all have four eyes, two in the front and two in the back. On this planet a creature is born with a handicap. Instead of being born with four eyes, he has only two eyes in the front. They all feel so sorry for him. He is intelligent and handsome. They could help him out and create a car for him with rear-view mirrors. But nevertheless, everyone looks at him with pity. Luckily, a plane from a place called Earth came to that planet. He hitched a ride back here, and he felt so happy!

If you are accepted as a father, as a mother, as a child in your family, you are so happy. If people turn their backs on you and don't accept you, you live your life as if it is a waste. We need to remember that happiness in a human life can be multiplied many times if we are accepted by our loved ones and family members. This is true both in family life and in society.

Society is like a mirror of our family. Whatever we put into society, society gives back. If we embrace our neighbor, our neighbor becomes our friend. If we can embrace everybody in our family, they embrace us. If our hearts are open, others' hearts are open to us. If we don't see this as our land, we feel rejected. If we contribute to this land, we are accepted. If we don't accept the land, the humans, the plants, and minerals, then *we* are the ones who suffer. If we accept these by opening our hearts, love flows from us to society, and then love flows back to us again. If we invest love into the family and society, we experience the returns. This is what karma is about. If we give love, we get it back. Love is a gift.

The greater the sacrifice, the greater the love. And it can start with us. We can cultivate love so that it flows out of our hearts.

Here is a funny story. There is a woman who lives in a neighborhood but she is very private. She doesn't care for her neighbors and doesn't interact with them. One day she sees a fire in one of the other houses. She knows there is a child who lives there, that she is in the house, and that the parents have gone out. This touches her heart. She runs into the house and grabs the child to her chest and to her heart. Fire is consuming the house, but she runs outside and escapes death though her skin is badly burned. The woman becomes changed by that experience. She is transformed from someone who does not care for anyone. She found that she loved this child deeply, and she began to bring the child gifts, to visit her regularly, etc. Why did she change? She changed because she almost died for this child. She realized that she felt great love for the child.

It is the same for people who sacrifice a lot for their country. For example, when they fight in a war, they feel great love for their country. And in relationships, when our sacrifice for the other person is great, the greater our love for the other person becomes. Love grows with sacrifice. The more we give, the more we love.

But in sacrificing for our loved ones, there is one thing to be careful of: sometimes we cannot escape feeling worried and investing too much of our emotional energy in the outcome. If we do not experience what we believe is a comfortable return, then hurt feelings arise. This can happen not only with a person outside of the family but also with our children and our spouse. In terms of sacrifice, when we don't require a return, it makes us grow. The more we give, the more we have to give. Jealousy is absent. Hurt is absent. On the other hand, if we give a lot of love and expect a return from the other person, then we cause that love to shrink, and that creates suffering for the other person and for ourselves.

So there are two types of sacrifice:

1) Beautiful — love is a gift without expecting a return.
2) A sacrifice that has an expectation that if I give this much, I should have this much back — like a calculation. This is not real love. It is not the sweet nectar of our heart.

We must ask ourselves this question: When we give love, is it with an expectation? Let us ponder this.

The next point I would like to make is about the flowing stream of compassion. Love is a gift. For example, we are like a well. People come and take water from the well. The well just wishes that many people come to take water from it because then more water will flow into it. A true well wants people to take water without asking for anything in return. If there is someone for us to love, we should be grateful and thank him or thank her for making the water in our well more pure and more sweet. If no one comes to the well, then the water dries up. We should offer love and compassion from our heart without expecting anything in return from the person who receives our love. If we give love away without expecting a return, *we* actually are the first ones to reap the benefits.

Love has been inside of us since we were children. We are so lucky to have a mother to love, or when we grow up to have children to love. However, there is unskillfulness in us. We begin to expect a return, and we start to have plans and calculations in our relationships, and then our love shrinks and loses its purity. It then becomes an exchange, and that is when the gap between us and our loved ones grows and the communication between us and our loved ones fails.

This is a true story of a family who lived near the temple where I practiced in Vietnam. I could look out over their house from the monastery, and I would observe that family to see what I could learn from them. Once in a while, I could hear the child call out to the mom. The mom was a young woman and would be cooking or sewing. I noticed that she would be surprised when the daughter would say to her, "Mom, I love you," and then run off to play. I used to wonder why the girl did that. Now I understand that there was great happiness in that family. Can you imagine if your child would speak to you like that? That child didn't have a calculation or expectation from her mother. Imagine how happy that mother felt. Happiness is in the palm of your hand. But as time goes on, our minds become burdened by worries and calculations. Then it becomes difficult to find those simple pleasures and experiences of love.

The happiness is in the giver. The person who receives the love experiences the happiness, but it doesn't compare to the happiness in the person who gives. Let us aspire to cultivate our happiness. Why would we want to drown ourselves in our worries, calculations, sadness, fame, or position, when in fact happiness is right here, right in front of our eyes?

During our lives on earth, our greatest need is the need to love and be loved. Happiness is available to us from the day we are born to the day we die. It is natural for us to wonder, "Is this a person I am going to love and who will love me back?" We all have this same need. We want to love our children and for our children to love us. This need is greater than our need for the breath. Yet we don't enjoy it when it is available to us. Instead we allow our sadness and worries to interfere. We need to start over, and it takes a lot of effort. If we are able to skillfully nurture our love, then we will be the people with the greatest good fortune. I hope you are all happy.

Of course, there is one more question that is extremely important. How do we practice to cultivate the stream of love in our hearts?

I have a short story to offer. In one of the past lives of the Buddha, the Buddha was a monkey. He had a beautiful white coat of fur. A hunter tried to find ways to capture this monkey and his family to take their fur to make a coat for the king. The hunter climbed up the tree where the family of monkeys lived. The monkeys were really intelligent, but they were not able to escape the arrow of the hunter. The arrow hit the female monkey, so she took her baby monkey and gave it to her husband. The hunter picked up the female monkey, and she was suffering great pain. The baby monkey climbed halfway down the tree. The father monkey was running up and down the tree, and he became so exhausted that he died and fell down from the tree. So then the hunter was able to capture the baby in a cage. The hunter kept it covered and warm and gave the baby monkey good food to eat so it could grow. But all he heard from the cage day and night was a sad cry from the baby monkey. This went on for many days. Then one day, the baby monkey was silent. The hunter thought that maybe the baby monkey finally fell asleep. But the baby monkey had died by the bowl of milk without even drinking it. The hunter believed that the baby would accept living in a cage without her family.

Even if we raise our children in material excess, with beautiful houses and lots of possessions, they cannot grow if they are not loved. Love is something really important, more than food or drink or material comfort. This human heart has the intention of love in it. But we have become unskillful as time has gone by. Let us look into our own hearts and ask ourselves, "Has our compassion shrunk?" We think we love our children, and yet we place so many pressures on them. We imprison them with our love. Let us take a look at ourselves. In family life, let us look at whether we have happiness in our hearts. If it is spilling out, then wisdom is right next to it. Love and understanding are very important. With these two elements, our lives will be happy, and we can offer happiness to our loved ones. We all have the capacity to do this.

CHAPTER THREE
Meditation

*We think the Buddha is very far away and that
nirvana is something we have to struggle to attain.
But nirvana is right here and now-- in our
breathing, in our actions, in the energy of
mindfulness. When we are happy or sad and aware
of it, when there are discourses and we are aware
of them, that is nirvana.*

Praise to Shakyamuni Buddha, the Fully Awakened
One.

There were special characteristics of the Zen
masters in the olden days. Here is a story from the
Zen forest circle about a disciple of Master Lin Chi.
The story involves a fire that was approaching the
Zen Master's hut, but the fire hadn't reached his hut
yet. His disciple ran in and said to the Zen Master,
"Why haven't you escaped from the fire?" The Zen
master said, "Get out of here!" So the disciple
picked up the Zen master and carried him out of the
burning hut. When they got away from the fire, the
disciple asked the master again, "Why didn't you
escape from the fire, and why did you tell me to get
out of here when I came to check on you?" The Zen
master said, "Life is impermanent, and if *you* die,
the dharma will not be able to continue."

Here is another story. A venerable came to visit a
monastery and the old monks went to meet the
venerable. They received him and invited him to sit
on a cushion in the ancestral hall at the altar where
they pay respects to their ancestors. There was a

small table with two small chairs. One of the old monks invited the venerable to sit with him at the small table in one of the small chairs, and he sat in the other. The two sat like that facing each other across the table for hours. They didn't do anything. They didn't speak. They just sat like that from dusk until after midnight. Then the old monk said to the venerable, "It's getting late, you should go home." So the venerable departed. Later, it was rumored that the two Zen masters had exchanged the dharma very deeply. How can we understand this story?

In the collective consciousness, we believe we have to "do something," for example drink tea, socialize, etc., in order to interact with each other. However these Zen masters were able to sit together without thinking, freely, for six hours, without doing anything. That is something wonderful that we do not know how to do these days.

For example, in the morning, I usually like to come to this meditation hall earlier than others before sitting meditation begins. People think I like to come in and begin sitting in meditation before everyone else. But really, I like to come in early before the others so that I don't have to say anything to anyone or greet anyone in the morning before I meditate. I am sure you can probably sit more peacefully than I can, because when I sit, an inner voice comes up in me. To be at peace is to be able to sit still and not have that inner voice come up. To be still and to be able to calm down is to be free without any discourse coming up in us. If we can do this, we can be a great Zen master like in the olden days.

What is the practice? There are many ways of practicing mindfulness. One way is sitting meditation. We live in a busy society, and it pushes us. We run after things all day, and in the evening it is difficult to calm down because of the stresses we experience during the day. We all have free time in the evening, but our minds are still stressed out. We come to Buddhism, to the practice, and our first task is to relieve our stress in our body and mind. Stress makes us fatigued, tired, and frustrated. When we are like that, we are like a bomb that is ready to explode. We carry around all the unrest we have in our daily lives inside of us.

The practice teaches us that there are dharma doors which are available to us for the purpose of alleviating the stress and anxiety within us. But only when we practice can we enter those doors and bring about results. When we have that peace as a result of our meditation, then we know our practice is effective. If we do not have that peace, then our practice is not effective.

When our friends come to the monastery and to the practice, there is a spiritual need in them. We need to help our friends to have peace and happiness. We all have a desire to make our minds and bodies lighter and to do it in such a way that our stress level is decreased. Concentration, mindfulness, and insight all support each other, and when we come in touch with the practice and actually put it into practice in our daily lives, then we can have insights and can realize something. But first we must calm our minds and bring calmness into our bodies. What I want to share today is how we can do this.

In our daily lives, we find it difficult to stay in one place all the time. We work, cook, etc. Even if we have a lot of time, we only sit still for perhaps a quarter of that time. In our society it is difficult to find time to sit still, so it's important to meditate during each of our activities. Our difficulty is that when we work, speak, or interact, we are not practicing mindfulness. I myself have been practicing for many years, and I try to be successful. Sometimes I am, but I came into the practice early in life, and my teacher never explained to me that this method was also a practice of meditation. He just told me, "You need to be aware of every action, placing down a bowl, picking up chopsticks, etc." I was so frustrated!

I was being observed all the time. When I was sleeping and placing my shoes down, I was being observed. For example, at night, when I was offering incense, my teacher would say, "That's not the way to do it." So I did it again, and he made me repeat it very many times until I could place the incense erect. He emphasized that the incense had to be erect for my mind to be alert, but at the time I wondered, "Where is the link between the incense stick and my mind?" I was really annoyed. He said, "Put all your body and mind into the act you are doing."

Imagine that when we would dry clothes, put on clothes, put on our shoes, we were reprimanded by our teacher. In one day I was reprimanded more than any police could have reprimanded me in one day! Slowly, though, I began to see that these practices helped my mind to rest in any activity that I was doing.

If we are not careful, we can be unskillful toward our fellow practitioners. For example, if the cushions are not straight in the meditation hall in the morning, inside of me, I feel some agitation. If I can use discipline to bring my mind back to what I am doing, it's good. But we can also be unskillful toward others and ourselves if we are always criticizing ourselves and others. This is not helpful. For example, in a family, let's say the husband is very orderly and disciplined, and no one else in the family likes to keep things very tidy. Then there are many arguments in the family. It can be like that in the monastery, too. The very disciplined monks can get frustrated with the unmindful practitioners. For example, there are special teacups made from glass here at this monastery. I see these cups all over the monastery. They have been brought here from France, and I see them left around all over the place in the garden, on a table, etc. rather than being washed and put away where they belong. That tells me that we are not being very mindful. We are living superficially.

There are countless things we take for granted. It's not that I care so much for things with material value (like the teacups). Rather, what bothers me is that I see that we lack mindfulness by not taking care of what we are doing at all times with our bodies, speech, and minds. In our society, many of our material needs are met, but we also must cherish the little things that we have so that we can realize our practice in every act that we do.

Every long journey starts with one small step, one turn of the wheel. Our peace and freedom start with picking up our chopsticks or spoon with mindfulness. Every activity in daily life is an opportunity for us to practice mindfulness. To drink tea or to eat with our body and mind in the here and now is mindfulness. To look at our loved ones with our eyes and our heart open is the practice of mindfulness. Do not look at them and think about something else. Why do we do this? Because we have the habit energy of our minds wandering off before our bodies. For example, our mind goes to lunch before our body, and because of that the present moments of our lives escape us. Life is made of this present moment, and the next present moment, and many present moments. If you are able to come back to the present moment, you can live your life in the here and now. If you think about what you need to do in the city while you are in the mountains, then you are not inhabiting your life.

We think of our past and future and take for granted what we have right now. Then before we know it, we feel we are being herded to our death, and we realize that we haven't really lived. We need to be aware of whatever it is we are doing in the here and now in each of our actions, not just when we are doing yoga or qi kong, but in every one of our actions all day long. For example, while walking, when we take each step, we know we are taking a step. When we look at our friend, we know, "This is my friend." In that moment, nothing is more important than that step, that friend, this cough. We bring all our body and mind to that small action, to that activity of our body and mind, and we bring our awareness to it. That is mindfulness. Does it sound easy?

It's not *so* difficult. To harvest the stars is difficult. To bring body and mind together in Buddhism is not so distant. The living Buddha and our teachers are only there to help us to practice and realize our awareness and to come back to our own lives. We each desire joy and happiness. If we go after fame or wealth, it is just to fulfill our desire for happiness. If we have not attained something, we think we are not happy yet. Many people have wealth, power, and fame, and yet they are not happy. Then they begin to search. But happiness is something within you, not something on the outside that you thought would bring you happiness.

When we are suffering and our bodies are not well, we realize how much our loved ones are there for us. No matter how much money we have, we realize that the thing we value the most is our healthy body. It's a wonderful awareness about our body.

And then we can realize something deeper. Emotions and perceptions can torture us when they come up, and that is not happiness. If we can realize a deep happiness within us and realize the things that make us happy and sad come and go, then we see that we can maintain our calmness throughout. We tend to look for happiness on a superficial level. But a deeper happiness is attained on a spiritual level when we can recognize the happiness within, and when we realize this, the longer it stays. For example, we can enjoy a good conversation with friends. But we can also come back to ourselves and give ourselves a happiness that is just as deep, for example by reading a book, lighting some incense, or taking a walk. Then we realize that *this* happiness is more stable, and we don't need to depend on any particular conditions around us for us to be happy. We can invite our happiness in and develop it within ourselves, and it can become more and more stable. All of us may have that desire. The happiness of the practitioner is to cultivate happiness in the here and now, and we can attain it by coming back to each of our actions during the day.

One day of practice with the monastics at Deer Park is not much. It is not enough to restore the energy expended on the other six days of the week. We only come here to soothe our anxiety, but we have to practice all the time so we can maintain our mindfulness through the day and throughout the week. For example, when we eat, drink, socialize, garden, when we are with our grandchildren or speaking with our loved ones, we have to invite the energy of mindfulness into every act of our daily lives in order to nurture this deeper happiness. Otherwise we get carried away by our daily lives. It is important to be able to practice throughout the day, every day. Imagine if we only practice two times a day, for example while chanting, or sitting, or offering incense. It is not enough. We are not worthy of the fruit we get if we just practice two times a day.

In the history of Zen, there are a lot of really good stories. This is one about the Buddha. When it was almost lunch time, he went to Ananda to put on robes to go out to the town for the alms round. He said to Ananda, "How do you put on robes to go out on the alms round?" Ananda was not sure and asked the Buddha, "I don't know. How do you do that?" Then the Buddha replied, "Just go out on alms rounds." As a practitioner, there is nothing mysterious about this story. Just let go of all thoughts of the past, present, and future, and just go on your alms round in the here and now. When we hold our alms bowl, we pay attention to our steps and don't project ahead to the next house. The most important thing is that wherever your body is, that is where your mind is as well. Whenever we practice, we put our entire mind into each act we are doing.

One day a venerable told his disciples, "Please come with me. I have a wonderful practice to share with you." He took them out to a farm, and he said to them, "Harvesting the wheat." He just spread his arms out like that, and they were very surprised. They thought he would share a practice with them so that they could become enlightened. But he just spread his arms out like that to show them the wheat being harvested.

We can interpret this story in two ways. First, we can say that perhaps the venerable might have taught his disciples this lesson another way. Perhaps he might have said to them, "Pay attention to each action you do" rather than waiting for an example of the reaping of the wheat to show them. Or he might have taught, "The dharma is within each person already and it cannot be transmitted. To bring our attention to each action each day is to water the seed of awareness that is in us already. To be aware of each action, we invite the energy of mindfulness into each action that we do. Then our bodily actions don't become heavy anymore. We are aware of them, and this mindfulness doesn't escape us." But instead the venerable in the story just spread his hands out like that to say, "I don't have to say anything else. To bring your mind and body back to the present moment is to bring your mind and body back to the wonderful awakened nature of our souls."

Now I would like to share some basic instructions for sitting meditation. There are many traditions that open many different doors. For example, one way is to put your hand on your abdomen and to feel the rising and falling of the abdomen. If you practice this, you calm and alleviate your mind and feelings when you are angry or worried. Pay all your attention to your hand on your abdomen and nothing is more important at that moment, not even the birth and death of a loved one. The most important thing is if we can do this for five or seven breaths, then we can make our stress, worries, and anxieties disappear. Stress is something that comes easily to us. Sometimes it makes us sick. To deal with our stress is to make our lives more fresh and joyful. When we alleviate stress, we have a lot of joy and happiness to offer to our loved ones. We know that in our family life, our times together will not be as good as they can be unless we can relieve ourselves of the stress in our minds and bodies. As we calm our minds, we can bring joy and happiness to our minds.

Another way to practice meditation is to pay attention to the in-breath at the nostrils and the air going out of the nostrils. Bring all your attention to the nostrils, and then focus your entire mind on your breathing. All of our bodies are different, so we can sit in different ways. We can sit on cushions, in chairs, or lean against the wall. We choose a position that is appropriate for our body. Whatever position, we pay attention to our breathing, the whole in-breath and the whole out-breath. At first we think the breath goes from our nostrils just to our lungs, but then we learn that it goes much deeper too. When we breathe with mindfulness, we can follow our breath to our toes and our fingers. Some meditators can even use their breath to control their body temperature and can sit in below zero-degree temperatures, and their nostrils do not freeze. When you touch them, you see that their body temperature is much warmer than your own. It's just by being aware of the breath. Breathing is much more powerful when we bring our awareness to it. Then we can bring healing into our bodies. This is quite easy to understand, and a lot of people have practiced and realized this.

The last dharma door is calming our minds down. Maybe we are not so used to the practice of mindfulness, and so our minds go in a thousand directions--east, west, into the past, always thinking. The practice of calming our minds does not mean that we cut out our thoughts with a knife. That is not correct practice. Rather, when we sit, we allow our minds to be free like space, and then when the thought comes in, for example about the past or the future, we do one simple thing and that is to recognize the arising of that thought. Then we can experience the most wonderful practice just as our ancestors have done, and that is to just watch the thought growing or diminishing, coming or going away. When the thought arises, it stays for a while, and then it goes away. Simply recognize it, but do not identify with it. It is not difficult to do, but maybe we are just not used to it yet. It takes practice. For example, a sadness comes up, and our tendency is to immediately identify with it and to think, "I am this sadness. This sadness is me." But to practice meditation, all you do is recognize it. "Sadness." Don't fight with it. Don't try to make it go away, just lightly recognize it. It's something so simple to do.

When we are able to recognize the feeling as sadness, something wonderful happens. We can recognize that sadness is an emotion that comes up in us but we don't have to identify with it. Then we don't get carried away. Many people today take their own lives and commit suicide because they feel so sad and do not believe that they will ever feel anything else but sadness. However sadness is like a cloud in the sky. It comes and it goes. We are not the sadness. Winds come and go, but we are the whole sky. Our awareness is limitless, infinite. We are not the sadness, the emotion. We are much greater than the sadness or emotion. We are the observer, not the observed, and we can restore our sovereignty over ourselves.

Emotions come and go, but we are infinite space. For example, it is like the people in this meditation hall. They come and go. The emotions come and go. They are guests who come in and go out, but we are the space. There is no sadness that stays with us forever, no happiness that stays with us forever. When we look clearly, we can recognize that the guests come and go, but we have our own sovereignty. It is this mere recognition that will open many doors for us and help us to recognize no-birth and no-death and how we can dwell in our no-birth and no-death nature.

In conclusion, I have shared with you three sorts of practice: being aware of bodily actions, coming back to the breath, and merely recognizing our thoughts. My previous dharma talks have explored more about the no-birth no-death theme in detail. To review, let me just say that we all desire great happiness, but to attain it we need to look deeply at the object of our awareness. There are things that come and go, but the observer stays stable. What is the object of our recognition? Everything we own or possess, for example our wealth, is outside of ourselves. Even our bodies, even our sadness, are outside of us. We can say, "This is my sadness, this is my happiness." When they come and go, we can recognize them and see that they are only a part of us, like a possession. But we are greater than all the things that we observe and that we own. Like when we watch a movie, we know that we are not the movie. Imagine all the discourses of our mind are just like a movie.

Who is the observer of the movie? Where is the awareness so that we are able to observe the movie? It's not from outside going in, and it's not from the inside going out either. When we are aware, then it is there. When we forget, it is not there. When awareness is not there, we are not alive.

We think the Buddha is very far away and that nirvana is something we have to struggle to attain. But nirvana is right here and now-- in our breathing, in our actions, in the energy of mindfulness. When we are happy or sad and aware of it, when there are discourses in our minds and we are aware of them, that is nirvana. For example, imagine a fish in water. Ask the fish, "What is water?" Why is the fish not aware of the water? Similarly, we are dwelling in nirvana already. And if you identify with your thinking, you lose your state of nirvana. But if you are able to observe and be aware of what you are thinking, you grow in nirvana. We and our ancestors are really not so different. If we are able to dwell in the energy of awareness, then we dwell in nirvana. If we identify with our thinking, we lose nirvana. The direct way to nirvana is meditation. That is the direct way.

KH'01

CHAPTER FOUR
Regaining Our Sovereignty

A spirit that is calm and tranquil is full. Just like the zero. The zero of our soul is a wonderful thing. It contains all the wonders and mysteries of the universe.

Praise to Shakyamuni Buddha, the Fully Awakened One.

External forces in our lives can cause us to lose ourselves to our conditions and make it hard for us to stop, to calm, and to come home to our true nature. These external forces can include the weather, people, conditions, and our own situation, and all of these forces can cause us anxiety. Whatever is outside of us and whatever is inside of us are interdependent. How can we practice so we can reside in our own territory? Our practice is to stop, pause, and calm our bodies. And this process gives us something wonderful—the ability to dwell imperturbably and to experience happiness, regardless of what is going on outside of us.

If there are things that are not worth being anxious about, just don't worry about them. What do we have to lose? Animals aren't worried about making it through the winter. They can make it through the winter to the springtime. Yet we humans accumulate and store our worries and then become slaves to them, suffering deeply before we leave this body. We have food and money in the bank, so why worry? We all leave this life with empty hands.

Nobody lives for us or dies for us. This is certain. This is the truth. We are afraid we'll lose our beloved one, but we can't hold onto him.

We think that the more we accumulate, the better off we are. We also believe that we have to keep and store our experiences, memories, and thoughts in our consciousness in order to be important and worthwhile. But we tend to lose our clarity when our consciousness is burdened by all these mental formations. The fuller our consciousness, the more useless it is. A spirit that is calm and tranquil is full, just like the zero. The zero of our soul is a wonderful thing. It contains all the wonders and mysteries of the universe.

The zero-ness is what makes our lives meaningful. What is the definition of zero? Is zero the opposite of having a lot of stuff? What is empty and what is full? In a house, we can only dwell in the parts that are vacant. When it is full of furniture and possessions, there is no space for us to breathe. In the same way, we can only use the empty space inside of us, just as the empty spaces in the house are where we can reside. A true house has to have space for us to breathe, but the shopping sickness keeps us focused on material things that are so useless. For example, we have so many clothes that we never wear. Why? To impress our friends?

For example, in the country of Israel, there is the prime minister and there are many people who support the prime minister as he makes decisions which influence the politics of the country. But what creates the deepest power is actually formless and signless. It is the culture that can exert the most potential power in a country. But a culture can either destroy or unite a country. It is the same inside of us. In the vastness and immensity of our consciousness, the zero is there. The zero is a source of immense wisdom and understanding. It helps us to recover, to be the master of our territory and of the stream of our own birth and death. We can end the wandering of many lifetimes through accepting zero-ness as our true nature.

How do we come back to our own sovereignty? Recovering our sovereignty means that our sovereignty has always been there, and we have temporarily lost it. We can recover it and regain the power of the king or queen of our own internal territory. It is as if the officers have taken over, and we must regain our essential power.

There are two ways to do this. At the shallow level, we regain sovereignty by becoming the master over our body. If we cannot stop at the level of our body, we will not be able to stop at the level of our mind. We need to be aware of our body to later be able to master our thoughts. So the first level is the body. The first step is to always be mindful of our body and to bring our body, speech, and actions into oneness.

We have the conditions of happiness right now. We need to stop and recognize the wonders in our lives—the loveliness of our partner, the loveliness of our child, the loveliness of our mother, our father, our house. We need to stop in our breath, in our body, and in our mind. We need to light the lamp of awareness and not get caught on the hooks of our wrong thinking. Imagine an ox being pulled by the nose. We need to keep our lives in our own hands and not judge ourselves with the views of others. Otherwise we are like that ox being pulled around by our wrong thinking.

To reclaim and recover our sovereignty means to stop at the level of the body and mind with a view that is clear and quiet, awake, imperturbable, like a mountain, unable to be disturbed. Storms will come and transform the landscape into beautiful flowers, and we can be as light as the floating clouds because we have nothing to lose or to act upon.

In this life, what is most painful is that we don't know when we will die. There is uncertainty in the fact of not knowing when it will happen. But it is certain that we all will die. We all have to live, and we all have to leave this body. We need to let go of our anxieties while we are still alive.

Recently a disciple of mine called from Vietnam to beg me to return to the monastery in Dalat where I was previously the abbot. He begged me to return to the disciples there. I have been away for nearly five years. This disciple told me that if I did not return, my name would be taken off the records of the monastery, and someone else would become the abbot of the monastery. But then he said, "If you would return to Vietnam, you could have your monastery, your disciples, and your name." He said that if I stayed in America I would lose all that. That is what my disciple said to me recently on the phone.

I replied to my disciple, "I never thought of Dalat as *my* monastery. Nor did I think of the disciples as *my* disciples. When I was there, I lived and practiced with all my heart. Now in America I am doing the same." The disciple then asked about my monastery and disciples in America. I said that I do not have a monastery nor disciples in America. I said that I offer dharma talks and practice mindfulness and am very happy here. I said, "I intend to stay in America and to die here. When I do, within fifteen minutes, my ashes will be spread in the mountains, and that will be that."

We don't have to be very good practitioners. We just have to come back to ourselves and let go of what we have. Don't work and enslave yourselves to things outside of yourselves. We are all zeros, but zero contains all of the other numbers within it. It is full of every other numbers. Zero and the other numbers inter-are. If we witness ourselves with all honesty, then we will release our suffering.

Our children are not our children. They are not our flesh and blood. Try not to see your children as belonging to you. Our offspring have to live their own, independent lives. Our children have the right to be independent. They can face the storms of life and become independent thinkers. All beings breathe and think independently. We all have our own sadness, joy, and independent lives. People do not possess each other. Our sadness comes from our wrong thinking.

On a deeper level, how can we reclaim our sovereignty over the mind, over the sadness and joy inside of ourselves? How can we go through life with space and freedom? The answer is this: by thinking, "I am present." Then we don't have to suffer so much, and we can have mastery over our lives. When we are present, we can recognize what exists in our consciousness. For example, when we feel resentment, it is unpleasant. We want to get rid of it, to eliminate it. But we cannot eliminate it. We try to avoid it or distract ourselves from it, but neither method works. We must invite the resentment to be there, and we must recognize it without running away from it. Only then do we have a chance to transform it.

In our consciousness, there is no irritation, no anger, no suffering that comes about without an invitation from us. We feed and nourish all of them. We water and nourish our own anger, our own sadness. Who can save us? We have to save ourselves from these mental formations and it must happen when they first begin to arise.

Here is another example. When I was a young monk studying at the Buddhist Institute, there were monastic students in the classes, and there were lay students as well. There was a very lovely young woman who was in my class. She was very natural and tall. She carried a tennis racquet in her bag. She was very kind to the monks. She offered us candies, and once she asked me to write a Chinese character in her notebook. In my mind, I thought that perhaps she loved me. I thought that perhaps she offered me the candy and asked me to write in her notebook as a sign of her love for me. So I spent a lot of time nourishing these mental formations. But what would have happened to me if I had not stopped? I would have left the practice. When I was able to think clearly again, I could see that she asked for my help because she could not write Chinese characters herself. She offered candies to the monks because she was a friendly person.

When a misunderstanding becomes so big that it reaches an unbearable point, what happens? We have the right to make our lives happy, and we have the right to make our lives into a living hell. We are the creators of our own sadness and suffering.

We also need to learn how to treat our family members as the individuals that they are in the present moment. We need to relate to them in the here and the now, not as the whole of their past and our past with them. Then we can be in contact with the joys of life. Life changes in every moment. Every situation changes constantly. The stream of consciousness flows like a river. We also flow like a river. We are each a new stream in every moment. We are a constantly flowing stream. We need to learn to see each other and ourselves anew and to strip away all our previous notions and preconceptions. Then immediately there is happiness at a deeper level.

Our interior space is immense and different from the space outside of ourselves. We have perception and knowing inside of us. We can recognize when something is clear and tranquil in this moment. And yet our internal monologue erodes the energy of our mind. We allow our whispering voice to talk all the time, twenty-four hours a day, seven days a week, even while we sleep. Only when we can stop this whispering voice can we enjoy good sleep and feel refreshed and rested when we awaken. If we can stop the whispering voice, we can feel love and joy. If we cannot stop the whispering voice, we become worn out. Turn off the whispering voice and go back to your own quiet mind with awareness. When we can recognize our mental states, we see that we are not them. We can observe them. We can take a step back from these mental states, and then we can reclaim our sovereignty at the deepest level.

Here is an example from the Avatamsaka Sutra. A woman approached the Buddha and said, "Dear Buddha, I have experienced enlightenment! I see the flowers glowing with light! The sky is glowing with light!" The Buddha pointed to some sewage on the ground and asked her, "How about that poop over there? Is it glowing with light too?"

Can you see the light in everything? This light is the light of your own mind, not the light of the sun or the moon or the stars. Stop giving rise to the whispering voice. Just recognize things as they are, without any commentary from the mind. This is the meaning of the story about the woman seeing the light in everything. That is why her teacher asked her, "Your sewage, is it giving off light too?"

The recognition is clear. Don't give rise to the whispering voice. The whispering voice makes us lose the light of the Buddha, the quietude, the clarity and the awakening of the mind. If we can do this one thing, we don't need to hate, to misunderstand, or to be caught by anything. This is how we reclaim our sovereignty. This is all we need to do. From this place we can respond to life as it is, appropriately. Then we are in sync with life. Let go of your consciousness, let go of your anxiety. Reclaim your sovereignty.

KH'05

CHAPTER FIVE
Our Purpose in Life

Where is our truest home that we can return to and where we can live in peace?

If you go deep inside, there is a great fortune inside of you for you to steal.

Praise to Shakyamuni Buddha, the Fully Awakened One.

I would like to share this line of a poem: "The gate is always open but no one enters it." To which the Zen Master, the Fifth Patriarch, replied, "You have to understand for yourself. Nobody can explain it to you." As I drink my tea, I think about this poem.

Today is Easter Day, and the theme of Easter is resurrection. Resurrection means that we remember to be mindful. Then we can bring lightness to ourselves and make life fully available, many times a day. Our daily practice is not so difficult. We invite mindfulness to be present, and this enriches our life. Truth has no name. We need to have the wish and the desire to practice. We need to have strong determination in this worldly life or we'll never succeed in the practice of mindfulness. We cannot make progress in the practice without these qualities. Our goal in mindfulness practice is to have peace and happiness, and this is something we can cultivate in our daily lives. We all have ups and downs on the path. But if we don't have peace and happiness, we don't have anything. Many of us have risked our lives to leave our homeland of

Vietnam to come and live in America, but are we happy? We have changed our lives to look for better material lives, for example after the war in Vietnam, but are we happy?

We must ask ourselves this: How are we investing our energy in our lives? Is it worthwhile to spend so much energy and time in the direction in which we are going? We are busy, searching, struggling to advance our careers to have better lives. Is it worth it? Sometimes we spend all of our energy to succeed materially. Is it worth it?

In the Dhammapada, there are these questions: What is achievement? What is enlightenment? After the Buddha's enlightenment, he came back to be an awakened person in the world of *samsara*, in the world of suffering. He was disappointed when he arrived in the heavens because he didn't want to be born in the heavens. He wanted to help living beings here on earth. That was his goal.

Now we have to ask ourselves: What is our goal? How do we want to invest our life energy? Is it worth it to invest all of our life energy in our personal success and career?

To have a human body is a great opportunity. However, no human body lasts forever. When it gets old, we can't replace it. And yet we exhaust our human bodies. We enervate them. But ask yourself this: What is the goal of my life? How do I invest my energy in my life? Please ponder these questions and find the answers.

Each one of us has a different goal. But we all have a common wish to be happy and peaceful. The greatest happiness of our human life is to have a human body and to be healthy. We may be willing to go through hardships in order to achieve something. But do we sacrifice our health and happiness in the process? Many of us experience despair, confusion, and worries. Our thinking wears us out. Is it worth it to invest our life energy in this direction? Sometimes we answer, "Yes, it is worth it."

Looking deeply, we can see that our worries and anxieties are created by us, not by the environment. Different people can exist in the same environment and under the same conditions, and some will be exhausted while other people can remain very free in the same situation. It is our mind that determines our experience. When we can change our mind and our perceptions, we can reduce our fears and our worries. Nobody can help us with this. We alone make ourselves worried or anxious. But if you know how to treasure your life, then you will find time to relax your body and mind.

We may never have this human body again. Let us discover peace. The moment when we let go of our anxieties, we can feel the joy and happiness that arise in our bodies and minds right away. That is the moment of resurrection. For us to be able to experience and dwell in that lightness and happiness is the goal and purpose of our lives. When we know how to rectify our situation and enrich our lives, then we can experience a small enlightenment. In the language of Zen, we call this, "Enrich and let go." Let go of worries. Open our minds. Then we are able to live our lives deeply. We are alive again. We alone can make ourselves alive again, or we can live as a dead person.

The definition of forgetfulness is: Whenever the mind leaves the body, then we are a dead person. Look back into your daily lives and ask yourselves, "Am I a dead person or a living person, walking on this earth?" We know we are alive when our body and mind are united. Look into the moments when your body and mind are together. We all experience a few moments like that. How can we live in the present moment? Are we mindful from morning to nighttime? Do we ask ourselves these questions?

How much time do we spend each day when we are alive, and how much time do we spend when we are forgetful? Where is our true home where we feel comforted and loved? Where are we accepted by the people around us? Outside of ourselves there is no real home, because everything comes and everything goes. This is very paradoxical. Sometimes we have a lot of difficulties, and we are unhappy. We live with so much suffering and difficulties, but people look at us from the outside and think we are happy. We cannot find our real home outside of us. Our real home is inside of us. We have to look inside of us and come back to ourselves, and then we find that we have so many habits, like the habit of being happy and being sad. These emotions and illusions are not our true home. The talking in our mind is not our true home. Where is our truest home that we can return to and where we can live in peace? Sometimes we live our lives like a sleepwalker, living in forgetfulness. It requires a lot of determination to return to your true home.

Here is a story about a conversation between a Zen master and his student. The Zen master asks, "How long does your happiness last when you steal something valuable from somebody else?" The student answers, "If it's a small thing, it lasts a little while. If it's a big thing, it lasts a long time." The next question the Zen master asks is this, "Think about the most precious and valuable thing you could steal. How long would the happiness last if you stole that thing?" The student answers, "Three days." Then the Zen master replies, "You might risk your life and go to prison for a happiness that would last for only three days? I am able to be happy for so much longer than that." The student then asks, "What is it that makes you so happy?" The Zen master replies, "I am able to be happy for my whole life." The student asks, "Please teach me so I can be happy for my whole life." The Zen master says, "You'll make your friends jealous if you are happy for your whole life. Do you understand?" The student says, "No." Then the Zen master replies, "If you go deep inside, there is a great fortune inside of yourself for you to steal."

How can we understand this story? We have a tendency to place a goal ahead of ourselves and then to run after it. In doing so, we set up a temporary home on the outside made up of wealth, possessions, titles, positions, fame, pleasure, etc. But our true home is deep inside of ourselves. We have to steal it, which means we have to crack open our hearts and seize the treasure inside of us. Then we can come back to ourselves, and we can be happy. We have to come back to ourselves in order to discover our true home.

In conclusion, we invest a lot of our energy in a goal that we believe will bring us peace and happiness. But our goal is fragile, and we just imagine that it will bring us these treasures. Many of us have risked our lives to cross the ocean to reach the Promised Land. Then one day we will have to leave this world. There is not a single thing we can take with us. It is wasteful to invest our energy in these false goals. We have to come back to look at ourselves so we can be really, truly happy. What is a really worthwhile way for us to invest our life force?

We don't know when we will be cremated and our ashes distributed on the mountain or in the cemetery. Can we lighten up now? If our intention is to go home, to go back to ourselves, then we can say we are really living our lives. Ask yourselves: Have I really come back to my home to become a thief of my own treasure in this life?

One day we will all have to let go. When you die, no matter who you are, you can't take anything with you, even your body. But if we are mindful enough, we can enjoy the true happiness that exists inside of us. If not, our lives are a waste. We have responsibilities to our country and to our families, but these don't begin to compare to our responsibilities to ourselves, to our own joy and our own happiness. The gate is always open. Are we able to walk through it?

CHAPTER SIX
Life, Death, and Karma

If we can see that this life is a precious gift, then we won't be afraid of death when our time comes.

Happiness and joy are in our own hands if we can nourish our practice of mindfulness as human beings.

Praise to Shakyamuni Buddha, the Fully Awakened One

I would like to share with you Verse 41 from the Dhammapada:

> *Whoever knows all his past lives,*
> *Sees both the happy and unhappy realms,*
> *Is free from rebirth,*
> *Has achieved perfect insight,*
> *And has attained the summit of the higher life,*
> *Him do I call a Noble One.*

When these teachings were given to an ill venerable by the Buddha, they helped him to attain arhatship and to experience nirvana before his body died. We must keep in mind that for each of us, this body will eventually go back to its true nature and to the earth, and we will have to return our useless bones. But our true essence will continue to return on this earth. Before we die, let us think about something simple that we can accomplish in this lifetime. For example, we can think about "Happiness in life," or "A heart that is pure." If we can see that this life is a precious gift, then we won't be afraid of death when our time comes.

I'd like to share the following with you today: All humans are afraid of old age, sickness, and death. It is important to recognize our fears, for they are a normal part of being human. We all have to die. We all go through this. This is normal. We all come and we all go. I have come and I have gone so many times. We all have come and gone and been here for many lifetimes, however most of us just don't remember it very clearly. But there are some who can. For example, the Dalai Lama knows that he has returned thirteen times. He even has the wisdom to be able to say, "In the next lifetime, I will return in this village, in this house, with this name."

Because we have died many times in the past, there are seeds containing these memories of our past deaths in our store consciousness. It is like when you cut yourself on a knife or burn yourself on a stove. You remember that experience and perhaps the pain. We may remember these deaths, and therefore we might be afraid of experiencing death again. But on the other hand, our soul never dies and has never been born. Even though our bodies have died, in our hearts we hold the wisdom that our souls have never died and will never die. We have never died, even though we don't believe this sometimes.

Our karma pulls us in certain directions based on our thoughts, words, and actions. Karma is another word for our habit energy. We can say that there are three levels of existence: the heavenly realms, the human realms and the animal realms. In this lifetime, we can see a manifestation of these realms in our own lives, and this is true in each lifetime. For example, a person full of hell always experiences resentments, anger, greed or envy. But heaven and hell are not just outside of us, they are also inside of us if we allow our mind to follow the tracks of our habit energies. For example, if we live a good life and engage in wholesome activities, then we will be surrounded by good karma. If, for example, we are a teacher, then no matter what we do, we will teach. If we engage in unwholesome activities, then whatever we do we will behave in unwholesome ways. If you are a person who kills animals, whatever you do, you will kill animals. But once you can control your habit energies, then you are a free person.

Karma follows you and never loses its seeds, for we are made of non-self elements. They can remain buried in our store consciousness. But nevertheless we can still be the masters of our own lives and not give them the opportunity to manifest. Happiness and joy are in our own hands if we can nourish our practice of mindfulness as human beings.

On the other hand, we can make our life go downhill by nourishing jealousy, craving, resentments and anger. And if we do, no one on earth can help us if this is how we spend this lifetime. No one else can control you. Sometimes we believe that it is really other people who pour gasoline on our flames, and then we blame them for nourishing our anger. But if we know how to control our minds, then we won't nourish our own anger regardless of the external circumstances. Each day, no one is behind you controlling your thoughts and feelings. No one is watching you and saying, "Don't act out your anger." It's all up to you. You may go to a new body, through cycles of birth, death, birth and death, but still no one is in back of you.

This is why we say, "There is no self and no non-self." Even though there is no non-self, there is a pure nirvana element in all of us. In other words, we are the water, not the waves. Karma is only a shadow of our true nature. Form contains formlessness. The truth of the form is the empty space within. For example, the useable and meaningful part of this meditation hall is the space inside of it where we can walk or sit. The building is the form, but what it contains is the empty space that we can use for our mindfulness practice. In the same way, our body is just like a meditation hall. It is the form, but it has to have a space inside of it for it to be useful for our practice. In order to maintain our internal space, we have to know how to breathe in and out consciously. We need to continuously nourish the interior space in our mental consciousness. When thoughts flash in front of us, we must allow them to come and go so other thoughts can be present. We cannot cling to them. If we have space, we have the ability to see these things clearly.

In the same way, the more love you have, the more your compassion can grow. If your mind is clogged up with sadness and other mental formations, there is no space inside of you to develop compassion, gratitude and love. Space means to have a mind that is clear, sharp and miraculous, so that happiness and sadness can be free to arise and then to dissipate.

Space means that we can reflect on ourselves and on the truth that this body comes and goes. These thoughts come and go. These feelings come and go. Even sadness and happiness come and go.

Everything comes and goes except for our capacity to touch mindfulness and nirvana.

We all have nirvana in our own hearts. What does nirvana mean to us? What is our Buddha nature? What is our true self nature, our true essence? I know an eighty year old lady who has a picture of herself as a twenty-one year old woman. What is her essence whether she is twenty-one years old or eighty years old? This essence is present in all of us in the present moment. If you see the waves in the river as high and low, you can become caught in your attachment to the form of the waves. But what about the water, which is always present? In the same way, the face of a person changes over time. The waves come and go. But our true nature, our essence, like the water, is always there and depends on our spaciousness. We are nirvana. We are our own true nature, our Buddha nature. Our joys and sadness are not us. Our feelings and thoughts are not us. We have not come, and we have not gone.

Meanwhile, the whispering thoughts go on and on within ourselves — commenting, observing and judging. Our thoughts and the whispering voice are running in the store consciousness. With mindfulness, we try to become aware of what is floating up. There is always thinking. Are we mindful of our thinking or caught in the thoughts? Are we living our lives, or are we just existing on automatic pilot? If we can be mindful of our thoughts, words and actions, then we are the sovereign of our own lives. We try to master the moments of our lives. We can use the practice of mindfulness to control our actions, our movements, our bodies and the things that come and go.

If we go deeper down, we can have faith in this understanding that all feelings come and go. Anything that comes and goes cannot be the totality of who we are. All we need to do to touch nirvana is to be aware of what comes and goes and of what does not come and go. Mindfulness is always there, has always been there, and will always be there. That is all. That is us.

Mindfulness can always be there, just as the awareness of what we are made of can always be there. What we are made of is the no-coming, no-going nature, our true nature, our true self. Behind all the joy and sadness of our daily lives is mindfulness.

Do thinking and feeling have form? A poem is there in our consciousness before it comes out in words. Formlessness is there before form. With our practice, we can go deeper inside ourselves and look at those whispering thoughts. We can be the observer and not the observed. This is how we become our own master, by becoming aware of all of our thinking. You don't have to do anything else. Just look around and recognize what is there already.

For example, I can look around this room and recognize the people sitting here without the whispering voice commenting. I can just see the people and be aware of the people. This is how we practice. We see without commenting, without getting caught. You have this ability to merely recognize what arises in your interior landscape. You have this ability to be aware too. This is the true nature of nirvana. This we know. We can say that we have never died because we are bigger than all our little, unnecessary thinking. When we grab onto our true self with confidence, then when we are faced with sickness, old age, and death, we have a direction to go in. We can give all of our hearts to our lives, to everyone, and to the earth. And then when we come back, we will be something of value that can continue on in each present moment.

CHAPTER SEVEN
Gratitude

I offer you a handful of diamonds. Your house, your children, the water, your shoes, your breath, each is a diamond. I have given you a handful of diamonds. May you reflect on how they sparkle day and night.

Praise to Shakyamuni Buddha, the Fully Awakened One

Earlier today we enjoyed a ceremony paying gratitude to our ancestors and parents. This is a tradition in the East, to pay gratitude toward parents who have passed away and to parents who are still alive. This continued when Buddhism moved from the East to Western parts of Asia and is often practiced at the end of the Rainy Season Retreat, which lasts from the full moon of the fourth month to the full moon of the seventh month on the lunar calendar. We show our gratitude on the last day of the Winter Retreat, which is a joyous day for the monastics because that is when our number of years as a monastic is counted.

In 1967, Thích Nhất Hạnh wrote a beautiful poem in gratitude for his mother, *A Rose for Your Pocket*, and we feel moved each time we read this poem. Also, this started a new tradition, what we call the Rose Festival, which is now practiced in many temples in Vietnam and in America. During the Rose Festival and similar ceremonies, we pay gratitude to our parents. Today I would like to talk about the meaning of the ceremony we enjoyed earlier today.

This morning, when we re-read *A Rose for Your Pocket*, the words in this small booklet touched the strength in our hearts. We felt touched, especially those of us whose parents are gone. A love for a parent is basic to our nature, and a love from a parent to a child is sacred and can be seen in both the human and animal kingdom. We express our love from child to parent and from parent to child. Because of the daily pressures and stresses in our lives, we sometimes forget that we have these two wonderful sources of happiness if our parents are still alive. But suppose they are gone. Your heart would ache. We often do not appreciate how lucky we are when our parents are still with us on this earth.

I called my mom in Vietnam recently and I asked her, kind of joking, if she's afraid of death. She said, "Of course I am." Then I began to wonder, "How would I feel if my mom passed away?" As monastics, our love for our parents is somewhat lighter than that of our lay friends. We know that our parents in this life are just for this life, but we also see that we have had many, many parents in other lives. Our gratitude radiates to our parents and also to all beings — for our clothing, for our food, for the tree that gives us shade. Our gratitude is shown for everything. But when I thought of my mom passing away, my heart still ached. In our lives, we have memorable moments about our parents and our childhood. Even if we are old we still have lots of beautiful memories. If we are able to bring up fond memories of our parents from our childhood, then naturally gratitude will arise. If there's no gratitude or love in your heart, you will be so unfortunate and feel restless. The first teaching on love is about love for our parents.

For example, I have a memory of my mother carrying me to a medicine man when I was ill as a boy. There were no hospitals or doctors near the village where we lived. We did not have a car, so she picked me up and carried me to get help. When I recently spoke to her, I asked her if her hair is all white now, because I have not seen her in quite a while.

Here is another memory I have of my mother. In 1975, after the North had taken over the South, after so many battles during the war, there were many misplaced people. After ten years of practicing as a monk in the temple beginning in 1965, I came back to visit my mom. On my way, I saw many dead bodies all over the place, and there were a lot of weapons all around, too. I saw death come to so many people so easily. I myself had not realized how important family was until that time. So I went to the countryside to see my mom. I had to cross many rice fields to get to my home. Because I was the only one from my village who was ordained as a monk, when the people in the area saw me coming, they knew it was me, and they ran to inform my mom. Then, as I was crossing the rice fields, I saw this old woman running toward me. She was running and then would fall, then get up again and fall, and get up again and run toward me. When we got to each other, she didn't dare hug me because I was a monk, and at that time it was not considered appropriate for women to touch ordained monks. Unfortunately, we didn't know about hugging meditation at that time. So I was just standing still.

She said, "I can't believe you are still alive!" And she cried and cried.

Here is an old story. There was a hermit who said to a man, "If you want to find the Buddha, it's not easy, but I can show you how to recognize the Buddha. Look for a person with a blanket around him and shoes on the wrong feet." The man left the hermit and went home. When he got there, his mother had put a blanket around her and was wearing mismatched slippers. He exclaimed, "I can't believe the Buddha is actually in my house!" Similarly, I had this realization when my mom ran and fell and ran and fell. That gesture represents the gesture of a parent who has so much love for her child. If your mom is still alive, she looks at you as if you are still a little child. Your parents raise you and cultivate love in you. They cultivate spirituality in you. There are many sutras that describe filial piety. Even the Buddha came back to be with his father when his father was ill. He taught his father to breathe in and out mindfully. He helped his father attain one of the four levels of meditation before his father died.

We are lucky if our parents are alive. It is important for us to visit our parents and spend time with them. By doing so, we fill the reservoir of compassion in our hearts when we show love to them. We can also do this by showing gratitude to our ancestors who have passed away. How do we do this? Our mind can be very strong, but our mind is intangible, and it doesn't need signals like a radio or TV to transmit information. The mind is alive and can affect another person directly, from mind to mind and from heart to heart. When we send kind and compassionate energy to others, they can feel it. The most subtle level of our being is the mind, our thinking, and the force or the ability to recognize what can touch our loved ones. We can use our thinking, but if we can use a more subtle level of our being, the connection is very powerful. The energy of our heart and mind is very strong. If we send love to a person, they can feel it. Even if their body is gone, their deeper levels may still be present, so we can send our love to them. Whether your loved ones are alive or whether they have passed away, send them the energy of your love and compassion. It's not hard. You don't have to believe in something superstitious. We can do this as practitioners. We can show gratitude to our parents in this life and to our parents in our past lives. This is a very beautiful thing we have the capacity to do.

This morning we practiced the Nine Touchings of the Earth to show gratitude and to practice this in our lives. Gratitude is a big aspect of Buddhism and is the basic teaching of the Buddha. And filial piety is the foundation of a person's character. If there's no gratitude, there cannot be love and compassion. So gratitude is a quality that we must cultivate. We must show gratitude to our parents, teachers, friends, as well as to plants, minerals, the sun, and the moon. All these elements come together to give us life. This is the teaching, and this is the practice we all shared this morning when we did all the Nine Touchings of the Earth — to the Buddha, the bodhisattvas, our parents and all living beings. Traditionally, we do this ceremony twice per month, usually in the evening. These nine earth touchings represent our gratitude toward everything in this universe. The more gratitude we have, the happier we feel.

This morning's ceremony was in Sino-Vietnamese (Hán Việt), so many of us, even Vietnamese speakers, did not understand it. So I will now translate a few of the Nine Touchings from the ceremony this morning.

The first gratitude and earth touching: All of us here, your disciples, practitioners, all of us, with one-pointed mind are addressing the ancestors. Or another way to translate it might be, 'We direct our attention to one source, on behalf of all of us being protected by the earth and the sky.' Or, 'The first gratitude is for the presence of life: the earth, the plant kingdom, water, animals, everything that is present. May we enjoy what life has to offer us.'

If we have gratitude, we will protect the planet. Ancient peoples, like Native Americans, lived in tribes, and their spiritual life was more evolved than ours. They frequently showed gratitude to the environment, to life, to the sun and moon. We might think they are very primitive, but their spiritual life might be more advanced because they have love in their hearts and gratitude. We in so-called modern societies might be proud of our accomplishments — conquering nature, science — but on another level, we are quite primitive. Do we pay gratitude to the sun that has warmed us, or to the moon? Over 80 percent of all poetry and art are created because of the presence of the moon. Buddha is also compared to the full moon. Mothers are also compared to the full moon. The moon is responsible for the cycles of living entities. The energy we have as humans is also because of the presence of the moon. So the first gratitude is to be grateful to the sun and the moon.

'We touch the earth to the three jewels in the ten directions.' Animals don't have the means to do that, so we do it on behalf of the plants, animals, and minerals. We can summarize this by saying, 'All of us are present here because of our wish to pay gratitude to the sky, earth, moon, and sun. We touch the earth before the three jewels in the ten directions.'

The second gratitude and earth touching: 'All of us are present here because of our wish to pay gratitude for the kings, governments, and founding fathers who have developed the country, for the people who were in this country first, for electricity, roads, and water dams far away from California.' Our presence here is not simply because of our parents but because of many generations of people who have built this land through civil wars and people who died to gain independence. The United States constitution didn't appear out of thin air. We pay gratitude as Americans and as people of this land. 'All of us are present here because of our wish to pay our respect and show gratitude to the founding fathers and ancestors of this land. We touch the earth to the three jewels in the ten directions.'

The third gratitude and earth touching: 'The third gratitude is to all of our relatives, our family members, and to everyone in society. We touch the earth to the three jewels in the ten directions.' Our direct support is from the people who live near us, for example people in our ethnicity and our family members. We cannot deny the protection and support of our neighbors, family members, and those who help us when we are in need. To be neighborly is very important. We show gratitude for the love and protection of everyone around us. We need the variety of all the different jobs people hold in society, including the culture of the society, the art, and the music that are created by humans.

The fourth gratitude and earth touching: 'The fourth touching is to show gratitude to the plant kingdom of the trees, the plants, the grass, the vegetables, the food that gives us life and also is the means of our transport, of our coming and going. Everything that makes up our life comes from our reliance on the plant kingdom.' There is a story of a woman who shows gratitude to a bus. Every time she travels anywhere by bus, she bows to the bus before she enters, and she bows to the bus when she departs to show her gratitude for the assistance of the bus in her transportation. To show gratitude to a bus, to a means of transportation is a way of saying, "Let us take care of it and treasure it. It carries many people across many miles." It is natural to have gratitude for a bus as a means of transport, and for everything that is present on this earth.

We can show gratitude for our food. We join our palms to show gratitude to the universe and to the cooks who offer us this food. This is a very beautiful practice, just as it is very beautiful for Catholics to cross themselves before a meal. Sometimes when I am out in a restaurant, I notice that practitioners are embarrassed to bow to their food in a restaurant. Why are we embarrassed to show gratitude for the food that is in front of us in a restaurant? What is wrong with showing gratitude in public? Some of us are very unskillful. Even we monastics sometimes do not show gratitude for the food offered to us in a lay person's home.

Showing gratitude brings you love and joy. The benefit comes not only to the object of our gratitude, but primarily the benefit comes to you. Gratitude produces love in *your* heart. When you have love and happiness in your heart, then you don't have to run around to find it. When you are filled with love and understanding, the joy will be there in you.

There is great value in cultivating gratitude. As humans, we are fortunate that every person is born to a set of parents. We learn love from our parents, so we all have the substance of love inside of us. We have to look back because society causes us to forget this, and then we think we need to chase after something far away in order to be happy.

What makes us most happy is love and the presence of our parents. Stop and reflect on the objects of your love so you can cultivate happiness in your heart and gratitude toward your parents, your partner, and your children. They all have the capacity to offer you happiness. Gratitude flows from you to your parents and from your parents to you, from you to your partner and from your partner to you, from you to your children and from your children to you. We can even show our gratitude even to our parents if they are no longer here when our heart is full of love. Let us not wait until it is too late.

So in summary, first, enjoy the happiness you have in your hands. Second, having a physical body is a great source of happiness. We'll have to let go of everything we treasure some day. If you have gratitude for your parents, then naturally you have gratitude for your own physical body and for your life. Don't abuse these. Looking deeply, you might see that you could be damaging your body, for example with worries, anger, and restlessness that cause wounds in your body, wounds in your heart and wounds in your mind consciousness. These wounds are very difficult to heal, and these emotions diminish our energy. If we know how to practice well, we will be able to stop the desire to run forward. If we know how to stop and be content with what we have and with who we are, we'll know how to lessen our own stress so we can sleep peacefully, enjoy our loved ones, drink a cup of cool water, and enjoy a bouquet of flowers. Yet the mind is caught in worries. We think too much. We lose many opportunities for happiness, for example like having gratitude for the presence of our parents. Be skillful and return to yourself and fill your heart with gratitude for your loved ones and your children.

Our children carry us into the future. They continue us. Of course, they owe gratitude to us, but we need to show gratitude to them, too. The treasure is in your hands. I offer you a handful of diamonds. Your house, your children, water, your shoes, your breath, each is a diamond. I have given you a handful of diamonds. May you reflect on how they sparkle day and night.

CHAPTER EIGHT
Successful Parenting II

As parents, you bring children into life. But you haven't automatically given them a spiritual education. Teaching them in a beautiful and wholesome way is the greatest gift you can offer. It is this that is the most beautiful aspect of parenting.

Most of all remember that all things become unpleasant or pleasant depending on our minds. If you see something as a source of joy, it will be.

Praise to Shakyamuni Buddha, the Fully Awakened One.

How can we learn and practice the dharma for ourselves and bring happiness to our families? If we have happiness, we will gain insight into how to raise our children successfully. Each child is unique, and as parents we have our own habit energies. How can we live our lives to the fullest? If we can do so, then we'll be able to teach the appropriate lessons to each of our children.

In Thailand, all children calm their minds in meditation for ten to fifteen minutes each day, and the government has now instituted this as a mandatory practice in all the schools in the country beginning in 2003. Thailand instituted this national education program after finding that one hundred naughty and delinquent students were able to be trained by Theravadan monks and were then able to return to their schools to become successful students. Like those school children, we too are fortunate to have the time to do sitting meditation to calm our minds. When our consciousness is calm, we have the certainty to take care of problems in our daily lives and to raise our children. Our practice becomes the foundation of our success in raising children.

It is interesting to mention that we have a four thousand-year-old Eastern tradition that indicates that we are already teaching our children when they are in utero. Everything that happens during the pregnancy affects the fetus who is developing there for nine months. Everything that happens affects their personality and we believe that the impact of these first nine months of development is equivalent to the effects of the next twenty years of learning after birth. So the personality largely develops in utero and is influenced by many factors including mother's state of mind and emotions.

Let us look at the difficulties in raising children. One difficulty is that we are responsible for the physical, emotional and spiritual lives of our children. If our genetic elements are not healthy, our children will have to suffer this. We are responsible for our children, and that is why we often expect of them what *we* want for them. However, this is unskillful, and our failures can result from us as parents trying to live out our dreams, lives and hopes through our children.

We need to ask, "How can our children be happy, fulfilled, and have spiritual lives? How can we train them so that they have enough energy to enrich their own lives with happiness from within? How can we enrich the beautiful and truthful qualities within our children so that no matter what their profession, they are happy?" This is how we should evaluate our success as parents. Please reflect on these questions.

There is an old saying: "You bring wood home, but this is not the hardest work. You make the wood into a table, but this is not the hardest work. You build a school, but this is not the hardest work. You have the children come to the school to learn, and teaching them properly is the hardest work." The greatest work is the work of a teacher. As a parent, you bring children into life. But you haven't automatically given them a spiritual education. Teaching them in a beautiful and wholesome way is the greatest gift you can offer. It is this that is the most beautiful aspect of parenting. In order to educate our children about their emotional and spiritual life, we have to be patient. We have to have wisdom and insight. And we have to build these lessons on a foundation of love and inclusiveness. Only then can we succeed.

We can also enrich our own lives through the way we teach our children. We can learn and practice in order to enrich their lives as well. Sometimes people ask me, "How can you know anything as a monk about parenting?" My answer is that I know from my own experience that when I was a young monk I was free to roam and study and practice without thinking about others. Then our consciousness changes as we grow from a bachelor to a father. It is the same when monks have disciples. We are thinking of them always. For example, if I am at a place where there are a lot of jackfruit or mangoes, and I would not lose face, I would ask to take some back to my disciples. We are always thinking about our children. So immediately your consciousness changes from one level to another level when you have children or disciples.

Let us be proud to have children to raise and to take care of. Parents are often sad when their children grow up and leave home. They have an empty nest syndrome. So if you have a little child, enjoy your little child. They will leave you soon. Enjoy changing their diapers, feeding them and dressing them. The connection between a mother or father and a child is very intense. The presence of children is the greatest thing that God has given us. When we have difficulties, we shouldn't make a big deal about it.

How do we transmit happiness to each unique child? We need to find the best way for each child depending on his or her character. But first we must look at the merit given to us by God in granting us our children and not complain. Our children nourish us in many different ways. Children, for example, nourish our patience. We become more fresh by learning to be calm and to be able to calm our minds in the midst of noisy and complicated situations, like the dining hall during the Family Retreat. If you can practice eating calmly while the children are crying and yelling and running around, then you can develop a thick patience that can serve you well in difficult situations later on. Family life is the best training ground. Be proud and appreciate how lucky you are to have three, four or even five children.

Most of all remember that all things become unpleasant or pleasant depending on our minds. If you see something as a source of joy, it will be. For example, a quiet child can drive you crazy if your mind is unhappy and wondering, "Why is this child always so quiet? What does it mean? What are they thinking? Why don't they say something?" Or you can train yourself to harmonize with the situation. That is the intelligent way to practice and raise children.

Regarding the gift of happiness, how can we enrich our lives in such a way that we give our children happiness, which in turn brings a gift of happiness back to us? It is easy to nurture happiness when there is loveliness in our children and when they respect us. But if you can open your loving heart to a naughty and difficult-to-teach child who still turns his back on you, if you can still love him even after he turns his back on you, then you are really opening your heart, and this is a gift! This is the great happiness of a Buddha.

There is a Zen story about a sangha of five hundred people. The monks begin coming to the abbot and complaining, "Today I lost a bowl." "Today I lost my sanghati robe." "Today I lost my chanting book." It turns out that one of the monks is stealing all of these items. All of the other monks complain to the venerable abbot and request, "Would you please kick him out of the sangha?" The abbot says, "Yes, I will help you so you can be happy." Day after day, year after year, this situation continues. Finally the monks come to the abbot with an ultimatum. "Either you kick him out or the rest of us, all four hundred and ninety-nine of us, are leaving the monastery." The abbot says: "You can leave. You are all so good in your practice and so gentle. Everybody will accept and respect you. You will always have a home. This other person, no one will accept him. So you all leave. No one else would possibly accept him, so he has to stay."

It is greater to love someone who is unlovable. It is easy to teach someone who is easy to teach. If you can teach and nourish a child who is difficult to teach, the greatest gift is the happiness in your own heart. The more difficult they are and the more we can teach them, the greater the happiness that we can attain.

As parents, we can either succeed or fail in the area of raising our children. Let's first look at the elements that bring about failure, and then we will look at the elements that bring about success. The process of educating children is not just a concern for parents. It's a concern for the whole community. We wish for the success of our children in our families and in the school system so that these children can later enrich our communities and society.

At the family level, there are so many conditions that bring about failure. First, if we impose our teaching heavily on the consciousness of our child, this can lead to our failure. It is comparatively easy to build a city, but to construct a personality or nurture a spiritual life takes a lot more work and time. To repair and transform the habit energies of a person is very difficult. Don't hurry to apply these teachings too quickly, because this would bring about failure. When we are anxious, we put too much pressure on our children. When we are ambitious for our children, then we are being greedy. But the path of education has its own plan and timeline.

Second, when we have a view or notion about success, for example to have a lot materially, to be well known, to achieve a certain position, or to own lots of possessions, these notions can also lead to failure. The views of a child are very different from our adult notions. Children seek the easy life, like to roam about with a backpack. But we exclude our children's wishes and desires about their lives when we dictate what we think their goals should be. Rather, we should rethink our notion of success and consider that real success is when a person has determination and strength to go through sadness and joy, to stand up straight, to be full of love and to not be afraid. If our children were to embody these qualities, we might find it easier to accept whatever career path or direction our children choose. Our internal sense of pressure would not be there, and we wouldn't keep trying to mold our children the way we think they should be. This in turn would lessen the generation gap between us and improve communication between us and our children.

How do we succeed in parenting? The conditions that bring about success lie in our way of teaching our children. In terms of the things we want to teach them, we have to be able to model those things ourselves. Look in the mirror. Children are very intelligent, and words alone won't work without your actions and without your personal example. We ourselves have to be able to do what we want them to do. If you create love and harmony, if you

can calm yourself, and then you can teach this to
your children.

For example, my mother had a habit of chanting a
litany of all my mistakes to me. Sometimes she
would sit me down for two hours and, as if reciting
a sutra, she would talk incessantly about my errors.
This is not good for the consciousness of a child.
Say something once or twice. That is enough. It's
not good for a child to listen to all of their errors.

If you have peace, you can be clear, and then you
can have gratitude for your children. When we die,
our children will continue our stream. We have to
thank our children. These children bring us joy and
happiness. Our children are not our possessions.
These children are valuable gifts. If we treat them
beautifully, then we will be able to teach them
without obstacles. Don't treat your children as your
possessions. Children are important members of the
family, and if you treat them this way, then they
will see that their responsibility is great. They will
understand that they are a part of the continuation of
our family. Let us view them as our friends and
allies. Then we can communicate freely and easily.
Pressuring our children just brings about more
failure than success, particularly when you see them
as an extension of yourself.

If our family is beautiful, we help society. If our
family is unfortunate, our child can do great harm in
society. The happiness of our child is determined in
our own consciousness, in the consciousness of the
mother and father. Inclusiveness leads to insight and
intelligence. When people are happy, they won't
give rise to crimes in the nation. The happiness of

each member begins in the heart of each mother and each father.

There is no gift we can offer to our children that is more valuable than for our children to be able to complete their own souls by developing spiritual lives. Then in turn, our gift to society is huge.

People are the masters of their own experience. If we create the conditions for happiness within our hearts, we can be happy whatever we are doing, as a king or as a baker. The same is true for our children. Therefore, the way we teach our children is very important. Please put more time into teaching your children and being there with your children.

CHAPTER NINE
The Energy of Avalokiteshvara

*Our sorrow, our suffering, our jealousy, we create
these for ourselves. They do not come from the
outside. If we are able to invite the energy of
Avalokiteshvara, it means that we are able to
recognize that all our happiness and all our sadness
come from our feelings. These feelings are changing
every minute, every second. None of them stays
permanently. Feelings come and go. If we are able
to call up the energy of Avalokiteshvara, then we
are able to eliminate all the suffering inside of us
because we recognize that the suffering is not us.*

Praise to Shakyamuni Buddha, the Fully Awakened
One.

Today is the closing day of the three-month Winter
Retreat, and I would like to share the following
experience. Sometimes I get really tired. But if I
have the opportunity to listen to three sounds of the
bell, to be able to listen to the dharma of the sound
of the bell, it is wonderful!

You may be wondering, "What do monks have to
do to get tired?" Well, there are days when we do
get tired. Imagine that on a Saturday afternoon, I go
out to a temple to teach and then come back. And
on Sunday morning I give a dharma talk here, and
at two o'clock in the afternoon I give another
dharma talk somewhere else far from the
monastery. In addition, many unexpected things
continuously happen during the day that we have to
respond to. On some mornings I transmit the Three

Refuges and give a dharma talk, and in the afternoon I do the same thing in another temple. Personally I find that nothing can make me more tired than having to speak a lot. And the most challenging thing for me is when I run into people that I know before and after my talks and classes. I cannot speak continuously all the time. It's kind of funny. So I have to reflect and look deeply into the things that I would like to share with them one on one. There may be old ideas I'd like to share, but I want to say them in a new way so that my friends can understand them. At times, when I am away from the monastery and I get tired, all I really want is to listen to three sounds of the bell to refresh my spirit. But it is difficult outside of the monastery, because the way they invite the bell at other temples is not the same as it is here.

Here at Deer Park we have a lot of time and a lot of conditions to practice, to listen to the sound of the bell, to look at our friends, and to walk during walking meditation. Sometimes, when we find that we are unmindful, we can rely on the collective energy of the sangha to help us return to our practice. That way it's easy. But when we are out in the city, it is very rare to have the opportunity to listen to the bell with a lot of freedom and ease and to just come back to our breathing with that sound of the bell. At times when we are really busy, when we are really tired, if we have the opportunity to come back to three breaths, that is a great happiness!

Manjushri said two lines that are quite memorable: "We have the opportunity to be still within one minute (or in one moment,) but that effort (or that

-128-

merit) is greater than the merit we would receive by building temples or doing other humanitarian work outside in society." Why is it that the merit is really great if we just sit still for a few minutes and bring our mind back to our body? When we look into our daily lives or our entire lives, we see that we have been dispersed. We have directed our energies outward, and we hardly ever take the time to stop and just enjoy our breathing and enjoy our life right in the here and now. If we were not lucky, then we would not know the dharma and would not know the way to come back to ourselves, and we would just spend our lives being dispersed and carried away by countless worries for others or ourselves. Even if we do have an opportunity to stop, sometimes we realize when we close our eyes that at the end of this life we cannot take anything with us. The only merit that you can take with you is to dwell peacefully and to sit with your mind and body in oneness. A peaceful mind is the only belonging that you can bring with you. So enrich your life. Even if we have to be very busy in our lives, we do have something that we can preserve for ourselves. That is the meaning of what Manjushri Bodhisattva said when he stated, "If you have the opportunity to sit still for one minute, then that merit is much greater than going and visiting the temple."

Here is a story about Manjushri. One time he manifested as an old man in Japan. Bodhisattvas can be very mischievous. He did not manifest himself as a monastic. He manifested himself as a prostitute in an area where many prostitutes were living. An old man knocked on the prostitute's door, but she refused to open it. So that old man wrote down this verse and he slipped it under the door.

"Why do you close your heart? Why do you refuse me? If I am not a monastic, if I am a normal human, will you still close your heart to me? I used to be a monastic. I wandered around to look for food. Now I ask you to give me one night to stay with you, so that I can sleep inside, but you refuse me."

The prostitute wrote this verse in reply. "I knew you as a monastic. I knew you as an old monk. You lived the life of wandering. But you know that this life, this *samsara*, is illusion. Many people in society are not able to see that this is illusion. But you and I know about the Mindfulness Trainings. And if you spend the night close to a beautiful female, then you may give rise to the mind of desire in this life." One thing we can do is to invite the energy of mindfulness to come up in us and to rescue us so that we can get out of this state of anxiety, of despair. That is the art of how we live this life. When we think about our desire to have pleasure, we can look and see that although this world is illusion, even so, we can live our lives with quality, with the quality of the practice. And then somehow we can wake ourselves up.

There is something special about today. Today is the day of Avalokiteshvara. There are three days each year when we offer praise to the Bodhisattva Avalokiteshvara. They fall on the nineteenth of February, the nineteenth of June and the nineteenth of September. Those are the days we praise the Bodhisattva Avalokiteshvara. Practitioners in Vietnam often chant the Universal Door Sutra to praise Avalokiteshvara. I would like to share how to use the energy of Avalokiteshvara in order to heal our afflictions.

Sometimes someone of nobility can really be disguised as a prostitute. The bodhisattvas in Buddhism are like that. They manifest in many forms. Avalokiteshvara can manifest herself in thirty-three different forms, sometimes as a child, sometimes as a prostitute, sometimes as a king, a monk, a teacher. I will not discuss this from the aspect of religion or faith. Rather, if you have a belief in Avalokiteshvara, it means that within you there is some wholesome energy, and that wholesome energy will collaborate with the wholesome energy around you. We find that if we have a wholesome energy in our heart, then we attract wholesome energy from the outside. For example, in the Vietnamese community during the time when there were a lot of boat people, they wanted to call upon the wholesome energy of Avalokiteshvara to help them. This means that we call on the wholesome energy within our hearts in order to heal the suffering both inside and around us. So this is, in a nutshell, how we can explain the Universal Door Sutra: calling on the wholesome energy within ourselves.

Many people know that Avalokiteshvara is the manifestation of compassion. In the Universal Door there is a phrase that says, "If you are being cursed or being poisoned, you just need to call upon the name of Avalokiteshvara, and then that curse or poison will return to the one who has cursed or poisoned you." So if someone is cursing or wanting to poison you, if we call on the name of Avalokiteshvara, the energy of Avalokiteshvara will help make those curses and poisons go back to the other person. If we look closely at this phrase, we will see that Avalokiteshvara doesn't really have any compassion at all. She is quite vile. If the other person curses and poisons you, and you want the curses and poisons to go back to the other person, it is really a pity for the other person, too. We need to acknowledge that Avalokiteshvara is the wholesome energy and also the energy of mindfulness within ourselves. We can explain the Universal Sutra from that perspective.

All things suffer infinitely, and Avalokiteshvara is there to help the world.

All beings suffer. If you travel around the world, then you will see that there is a lot of suffering. For instance, here in America we don't have a lot of material suffering. In America, even if you are really poor, you won't be starving or lacking as much as others in Third World countries. But still if we look at life here, from the rich to middle class to the poor, we see they still suffer a lot. If you don't suffer from a lack of material comforts, then you suffer from a lack of spirituality. In other words, if you don't suffer from lack of food then you suffer from the fact that your mind is always looking for something else outside of itself and in the future. When you can come back to yourself and recognize the energies within you and be mindful, then you can release yourself from suffering.

I know a Vietnamese woman who prayed to Avalokiteshvara to move her to America to be with her son. Then, once she came to America, she prayed to Avalokiteshvara to send her back to Vietnam. So I asked her, "Why is that? Avalokiteshvara is not so free to be able to help transport you from Vietnam to America and then back from America to Vietnam." She said that in Vietnam she may have lacked food and shelter, but when she came to America there was a great sadness. She wanted to go to America in order to spend time with her children. But they didn't have any time to spend with her at all, so she was sad in America. Her children work all week, and on Saturday they go out with each other. On Sunday they are free but they have so many things to take care of. In Vietnam, when she had free time, at least she could go to the temples, or when she stepped out into the street she could speak to other people. She said, "In America, I cannot say anything to anybody. I can't even answer the phone because I can't speak the language." So we can see that whether rich or poor, young or old, we all have suffering, and these sufferings will be released only when we can call upon the energy of Avalokiteshvara within our hearts. If we are not yet able to call upon the energy of Avalokiteshvara within our hearts, then there is no way that we can be free from our suffering.

Sometimes, when we are retired and our children are grown, we don't have to worry about earning a living or taking care of children anymore, but there is still a suffering inside of us. Somehow we feel the emptiness inside of us. In the Universal Door Sutra there is another verse: "If you are caught in a storm on the sea during a trip on the ocean, call upon the energy of Avalokiteshvara. If you are standing on the shore, look at how deep the blue water is. Imagine you are in a small boat on the ocean. Imagine the storm. How can you withstand the storm in that little boat?" Let's compare this to our daily lives. As I was saying, some days we feel the emptiness inside of us. We don't really have anything specific to worry about. We don't have to be busy, but sometimes when we are retired we are very lonely and don't know what to do. You open the refrigerator and you don't see anything you want to eat. You go around the house and you don't see anything you want to do. See how lonely we are? At that moment of the first suffering, without the energy of mindfulness, we feel very lonely, and we just want to cover it with something. And if you are not a very good practitioner, then you might just turn on the television and begin to consume all the poisons and toxins from the television set. That is one form of suffering. The other form of suffering is the thought that, "When we leave this life we don't know where we are going to." If we say we are going to call up the energy of Avalokiteshvara, it means that we are going to call up mindfulness so that we can rescue ourselves and live freely. With the energy of Avalokiteshvara, we don't have to be fearful anymore. Then we will know how to call up the energy of mindfulness to protect ourselves.

The Universal Door Sutra talks about a person who stands on top of a mountain and someone pushes that person into a pit. All the person needs to do is to invoke Avalokiteshvara's name and then that person is safe just like the sun hanging in the sky. I think many of us cannot imagine this, that you are standing on top of a mountain and someone pushes you down and you would not fall down. So what is the peak of the mountain? The peak here means success, fame and money. A person who stands on the peak of the mountain means a person who stands at the top of success and gives rise to pride and arrogance. Just imagine a wave that goes up must come down. So many people compete to climb up to the top. How can we survive if someone pushes us down? We cannot explain this sutra literally by saying that if you just say the name Avalokiteshvara, then you will be safe. What the sutra means is that when you invite the energy of Avalokiteshvara to come up inside of you, you begin to see that reaching to top will be inevitably followed by a period where we then go down. That is the first thing we have to recognize. In other words, there is no such thing as a wave that goes up without coming down.

Second, we need to understand that the desire not to succeed is also a problem. In the case of the people who succeed, they may give rise to pride and arrogance. But in the case of the people who do not succeed, they may give rise to inferiority complexes. So there are two complexes that exist inside of us that make us suffer: the superiority complex and the inferiority complex. If we look deeply, we see that the suffering does not come about because of whether we win or lose. That is just the outside suffering. But there is also suffering that comes about from inside of us. Our mind creates paradise, and our mind creates hell. We can come up to the door of paradise, but if we don't enter, then the door to hell opens wide and we fall right in.

There is a knight with a sword who stands in front of two doors. The master in front of the doors asks him, "What is your career? What is your profession?" And the knight replies, "I am a samurai." The master says, "You are not a *real* samurai." Because the knight felt suddenly insulted, he got really angry. Then the master said to him, "The door to hell is already open." The samurai was really intelligent, and he realized that he had been tricked by the master. The master saw this and replied, "Well, now the door to paradise is open in front of you." I offer you this story to show you how our mind can create our suffering.

To be poor is to suffer. Is that true? Nobody really can be called poor. Nobody really can be called wealthy. If the poor man looks down, he can see that there is always someone even poorer than him. And the wealthy man, when he looks up, he sees that there is always someone wealthier than him. So there is no absolute comparison. There is no way to compare how beautiful you are or how ugly you are. Look at me. How short am I? If I stand next to Thây Pháp Trí, am I short or am I tall? So from this point of view, we have to come back to our mind. Our sorrow, our suffering, our jealousy, we create these for ourselves. They do not come from the outside. If we are able to invite the energy of Avalokiteshvara, it means that we are able to recognize that all our happiness and all our sadness come from our feelings. These feelings are changing every minute, every second. None of them stays permanently. Feelings come go. If we are able to call up the energy of Avalokiteshvara, then we are able to eliminate all the suffering inside of us because we recognize that the suffering is not us.

Is it difficult to understand? I am aware that this is quite difficult to explain. I am teaching a class each Thursday, and we are studying the Forty-Two Chapters Sutra. I recently brought up this issue with the students in this class. I spoke about the five *skandas*: form, feelings, perceptions, mental formations, and consciousness. The Buddha called the structure of this physical body by the two names, *nama,* which means form, and *ropa,* which means mental. Form here means this physical body, and mental here means the mind, which refers to all the seeds from the past until now that we have collected in our store consciousness. The first thing we have to recognize is this body. We think this is our real body. But our body plays a very small role in Buddhist psychology. The remaining four of the five *skandas* — feelings, perceptions, mental formations and consciousness — play a much bigger part.

Sometimes our feelings can be very obvious so that we can recognize them, such as our anger, our sorrow and our jealousy. When they come up, sometimes they come up with images, and then we can recognize them more easily. However, perceptions are a bit more difficult to recognize than the feelings. Feelings relate somehow more closely with the forms. Our joy, our happiness, our sorrow is not purely related to our mind, but it also relates to our physical body. For example, when we look at a beautiful flower we feel happy. So the happiness is related to our eyes, or in other words, our form. But in the case of perceptions, they are purely related to the mind. When we call up the past, then we call it perceptions. Our mind consciousness is always moving. It never stops from one thought to another thought, from happiness to sorrow. The last *skanda*, consciousness, contains all the seeds that we store in our mind consciousness. Our store consciousness is full of things that we remember and whenever we see something that reminds us of those other things, our consciousness brings up these images from the past. These things then create our joy, our happiness, our sadness and could lead us to the six paths of wandering. To invite the energy of mindfulness means that we invite the energy of Avalokiteshvara to come up inside of us, and then we know clearly what is happening.

You may ask, "How does the energy of Avalokiteshvara relate to these things? If the energy of Avalokiteshvara is the energy of compassion and loving kindness, then how can we overcome and embrace all of the suffering of the world?"

First of all, I would like to share with you that the energy of Avalokiteshvara is not in this physical body, but it is also not outside of this physical body. For example, sorrow, sadness and joy are not this physical body, but when we become pulled away by this sorrow or this sadness, then we drown in this physical body. When we come back to ourselves to recognize the energy of Avalokiteshvara, then when we are sad or angry in the moment, we are able to recognize that "I am sad," or "I am angry." When we invite the energy of Avalokiteshvara to be inside of us, then when we are standing on the top of a mountain and someone pushes us down, we do not fall down. It is the same when we are able to recognize that our anger is our object, it is not us. When we look at a pen, then we are able to see that the pen is the object of our eyes. Often, when we are angry, we forget that anger is just the object of us, like the pen. It is being recognized by us. "This is not ours." So the anger is still there, but the energy of mindfulness permeates the anger, and the anger is diminished by that recognition.

Consider the energy of Avalokiteshvara to be like space. We call it energy, but in fact it can also be called our true nature or our Buddha nature. There are so many words we use to try to define this quality of being. Imagine the energy as space, and our physical body exists just like the universe within space. Imagine our feelings are just like the animals that exist on this planet. Our perceptions are like the people who are busy. The mental formations are like the clouds floating freely in the sky. And our consciousness, that is the dust in the air. The sun shines light on all of this: the planet, the animals, the higher species, and the dust in the air. All of it can be seen in the sunlight, which can be called the wholesome energy of Avalokiteshvara. We say, "We have a sadness. Anger is a feeling, a mental formation." When you are happy you are light. But when you are sad, you feel that you settle down. If you are not very skillful in the practice, you will be drowned in your sadness. But if you practice skillfully, then you recognize all kinds of mental formations. If you feel sad, you can just imagine yourself as a cloud in the sky with the energy of mindfulness like the sunlight that can shine on everything. Simply doing the recognition, which we call "the mere recognition," is to recognize all of the mental formations in us. When we are able to recognize them, then we are not pulled around by them into the realm of suffering. When we are able to live with that wholesome energy, then we see that our lives will not be drowned in sorrow or despair. When we bathe in that wholesome energy, then we end our suffering.

There are a couple difficulties we encounter as we practice this. The first difficulty is that when our mind has a happiness, or a sadness, or anger, then we often immediately begin to identify with that happiness or sadness or anger. We don't have the capacity to see that "This is our happiness, and we are the energy that can recognize this happiness or sadness. We are the energy that can recognize this suffering." This is our first difficulty, not being able to do that. When we have something come up in our minds, the most intelligent thing that we can do is to recognize it as something that we own. But we have the habit of saying, "That's us." We always identify ourselves with all of the sadness or happiness or suffering inside of us, and that is our first difficulty.

The second difficulty that we have is that we cannot bring our minds back to the present moment. We always allow our minds to go to the future or to stray in the past. This is easy to understand, because when we were children we were taught that life is something that belongs in the future. We always chase this life in the future, and when we become tired and we cannot chase after the future, then we remember things in the past and we drown ourselves in memories of the past. There are very few people who can stop and come back to the present moment and recognize life in the present moment.

The Buddha gave this example. Imagine a cart rolling on the road. Whether the cart wants to go to the West or the East, a long way or a short distance, the most important thing is that the wheels of the cart always come in contact with the earth. If the road was this long [drawing a line on the white board with a marker], the past was over there and the future is over here. We have so many people around us — our parents, our teachers, our society — and they all teach us that our life is in the future. We have to be good and diligent in our studies, and when we get our jobs we put all our lives into them, and we continue to chase after something in the future. But when the cart is rolling close to the end and we know that death is approaching, we keep thinking of the past. Our life existed in the past. We always think of the past, and we keep forgetting that if the cart rolls over there, the only way it can go into the future is to come in contact with the earth.

Whether we are a hundred years old or the age that we are right now, our life only exists in the present moment, right where we are, right now, right in the here and now. In this moment, with this breath, we can let go of all of our worries and anxieties. If we are able to establish ourselves in the present moment, we can allow the cart to roll into the future with a lot of happiness. But if we cannot do that, then we are allowing the cart to roll into the future with a lot of suffering.

Right now, if we are able to call the energy of Avalokiteshvara back into our hearts, immediately we will be able to let go of the sufferings and afflictions that we are carrying on our cart from the past. Life is only available in the present moment, that small moment, where the wheels come in contact with the earth. And we know that we cannot change our past, whether it is wonderful or filled with a lot of suffering. And our future is in the future. We cannot do anything about it. When we approach the future, there is another future ahead. Things change all the time, and we cannot know what will happen in advance. We know that life is only available in the present moment. And if we are able to call upon the energy of Avalokiteshvara to come and to help us to be aware of every single moment, then immediately we can let go and release all of our suffering.

Do you think there is any past, any suffering, any sadness, or any anger that is not owned by our mind? If we want to call upon a sadness in the past, then we have to use our mind to call it up. Our consciousness can bring up all of the past and think of these things. And if our mind or our consciousness is not whispering all of these things all of the time, then our past will not come up for us. For example, I could be very happy right now until someone just steps through the door and I remember that this person has caused me to suffer for many years. Then in my mind, the first words that come up could be, "Oh, him again," or "Oh, her again." And then we begin to recall all of the difficult moments that we have had with this person. So many things come up in our minds about all the bad things that this person did, and we become angry and frustrated. So we can see that all of the frustrations and anger come up because of these conversations and this whispering voice in our mind. We can continue with these conversations, and they can imprison us for our entire lives. Or we can call upon the energy of Avalokiteshvara and say, "Oh, I recognize this voice! I recognize this mental formation!" The energy of Avalokiteshvara is the mere recognition, and it is like the sun shining on something dark. You can do this. There is recognition without speech, and there is recognition with speech. We can just see, and we know. We just listen, and we hear. And this state of recognition is present with us right in the present moment. It does not arise from the discourses in our mind. The energy of Avalokiteshvara is the energy of mindfulness right in the present moment, and it is the ability to come in contact with the present moment, moment to moment, and to always have the wheels be in touch with the earth.

That energy is always aware of the five *skandas*: form, feelings, perceptions, mental formations and consciousness. We can recognize those things that come up right away, and it is like the light of the sun. It can shine into everything. Then we can recognize all of the seeds in our mind. It can shine on our consciousness and on all of the discourses in our mind that arise, and then we can recognize them right away. This recognition will help free us from the afflictions of the past, and if we are able to do this, we can carry a lot of happiness with us into the future.

In this moment we can recognize that we have a lot of baggage stored up in our consciousness based on what has happened in the past. But this baggage is not us. In the past, we have imprinted the images of those whom we dislike or our enemies very darkly in our minds. If we have the energy of mindfulness when those images come up, then we do not identify with that anger, frustration, or suffering. Immediately we can end all of our suffering of the past right in the present moment. And in the present moment, if we are to live with this energy of awareness of all of the suffering of our past, our cart can be very free. Our cart will be very light as it goes into the future, and immediately we can save ourselves and we can help many people with their afflictions as well.

There was a deva who came to visit the Buddha, and he asked the Buddha, "Dear Buddha, you live in the forest and you just eat one meal a day, but how come you and your disciples have a very peaceful demeanor? You don't seem to have any sadness or suffering." The Buddha answered, "It is because I don't regret the past, and I don't worry about the future, and I dwell in the present moment, and that is why my demeanor looks very peaceful." This means that Buddha and his disciples have that peacefulness, and it is because of their ability to dwell in the present moment. We can be fifty years old and very rich, but people may think that we look eighty because we worry too much about the future, and the weight of the past is on us. Either we run to the past or to the future. We haven't had the ability to dwell in the present moment. We don't invite the energy of Avalokiteshvara to come to our mind and to come to our heart in order to alleviate the suffering that we have. We make ourselves suffer. And each time a sadness comes up or a happiness comes up, we identify with that sadness or that happiness. We think that we are that sadness. But that is not the case.

We are much more than the sadness or the happiness that comes up. We are much greater. We are much more immense than that. Once the sadness comes up and we identify ourselves with that sadness, then we go down right away. Once the anger comes up and we identify ourselves with the anger, we are burned by the anger. If we are able to say, "Oh, this anger is my feeling, and I am the person who recognizes the anger, or the sadness. I am not the sadness. I am the one recognizing the sadness," immediately we can cut off all of the anxieties that we have about the past or the future and we are living with the energy of Avalokiteshvara. To live in that way is to have a lot of freedom.

I want to share a funny story. One day a Zen master entered a very long, deep concentration, and his breath was not present anymore. When his brothers touched his head and his feet, they were cold, so they thought he was dead, and they went to burn him. He wasn't dead yet, but he was just in a deep concentration. When he came back to find his body, he couldn't find it. So he kept calling on his body, "Where am I? Where am I? Where am I?" all over the temple. And the monks were so scared because they thought he had become a ghost. Everyone in the community was afraid. One day a woman Zen master came and she heard this story. She said, "Let me sleep in the room that belonged to him. I will cure this." Then she said, "Please bring a pot of water and some firewood."

That night he came and very tragically called out, "Where am I? Where am I?" because he could not find himself. His call made everyone afraid and their hair stand on end. The woman Zen master said to him, "I think you are in this fire." Because he was only consciousness, he didn't know what it was like to be hot or cold and couldn't burn himself, so he went into the fire but said, "I am not in this fire." Then the woman Zen master said, "Maybe you are in the water," and he went into the water and said, "I can't find myself in the water. I don't see myself." Then she said, "Maybe you are in the earth." And he went into the earth and couldn't find himself in the earth. Then she said, "Maybe you are in space," and he said to her, "I have already looked there, and I can't find myself there either." So the woman Zen master said, "You are of the nature of no-birth and no-death. Your body is just something borrowed. You can enter fire, you can enter water, you can enter the earth, you can become space, so why do you want to find this body that is so limited, that cannot enter fire or water or earth or sky?" This story is quite wonderful!

There is another story about a Zen master who would close his door whenever guests would come. When they knocked on his door, he would say, "No one is home."

The energy of Avalokiteshvara is not anywhere else but inside yourselves. It is the energy of awareness, of mindfulness. Awareness that is full of discourses within ourselves is of the nature of birth and death. Something that is born has to be subjected to death, has to be subjected to suffering, but something that is of no-birth and no-death is the energy of awareness within you. It is not transmitted to you by your parents or teachers or anyone, but you have had this energy for limitless time. The energy of awareness is not the things that we are being aware of. For instance, we can scan this room and see things. We can listen and hear things, but we don't have to have any discourses in our minds to be able to recognize what we see and what we hear. We have this gift; it is our nature. It transcends the nature of birth and death. It transcends age, and it can help us to get out of our afflictions and see that with this body we are just like anybody else. We still eat and drink. We do everything normally. But when something happens, we don't have to drown ourselves in that. We just recognize it. If our loved one should pass away, we don't need to cry. We see that it is only the body of our loved one that has passed away. And we are the energy that recognizes the happiness or sadness or that recognizes that inside of us there are discourses. All we need to do is to recognize that, and then we can cut off all of our afflictions. And I feel there is nothing more wonderful than to be able to live with that wholesome energy.

If we were to offer each other money or something material as a gift, then it could be used up. But if we can give each other this energy of mindful awareness, then our lives becomes an offering, because we are not carried away by our happiness or our suffering. We offer our loved ones our solid presence. There is something that I would like you to practice. When you are happy or when you are sad or when you are angry, then just say this to yourselves: "This is my anger, this is my happiness, this is my suffering," and do not say, "I am angry, I am sad, I am this, I am that." It is different to say "This is my cup of tea," than "I am this cup of tea." "I am not this sadness. I am the person recognizing this sadness." When we practice mindfulness, then we can be like the wheels of the cart that come in contact with the earth each moment, and we can live our lives deeply in every moment.

CHAPTER TEN
Happiness and Letting Go

Each day is a new day. Each breath is a new breath.

Praise to Shakyamuni Buddha, the Fully Awakened One.

Today it is very cold outside. Yet happiness is close to us and very simple. Our teacher the Buddha was able to dwell in peace and enjoy small happinesses and many happy moments. Yet in this time and place, we have so many creature comforts and love, but still we drown in unhappiness and sorrow. That is what distinguishes us from the Buddha. We are ordinary people because we cannot live happily in each moment and the Buddha is the Buddha because he could. That is the only difference. Our perception or how we look at life is what separates us from being a Buddha. And yet these two ways of being are very close to one another.

Let me use an example. In the morning as I walk to the meditation hall, I can see the lights of the city of Escondido nearby, as it is still quite dark at this time of year around five o'clock in the morning and the monastery is situated on a mountain. I also look down at those city lights at night. We must ask ourselves: How many times will we be able to look at this view of the city, at the beauty in nature, at our loved ones? How long will these conditions last before they go away? And do we feel these things are the things that we treasure most in our lives?

The first question reminds us that we aren't very skillful in recognizing and enjoying the things that we possess. We need to treasure the beautiful, wonderful, beneficial things we have in our lives. Instead, we get angry at our loved ones. Then we try to punish others. We plan cold wars with our beloved ones.

Instead, imagine saying, "I'm sorry." How would they feel? The beauty is in front of us, but we will lose everything we have abruptly one day. How long will we remain in this life to enjoy beauty and comfort, to live fully with our heart, to live fully with the person we love? How can we keep our hearts open so compassion can continue to flow? Let us not punish ourselves with worries, envy, and sorrow. We want to be here in this life a long time, so let's offer the best of ourselves to our loved ones. Let us do this.

This is a truth: No one knows for sure how long they have to live. When we look at a leaf, at the moon setting, breathing in the fresh air, let us remember that everything will fade and go away. If we keep this in our minds, we will know what to do to relax our minds and to lighten up. Then we will know what to do to be present for our loved ones. I know we can do it, right here and right now.

There is something else I'd like to share. We have wonderful, beautiful things in front of us. If we are skillful, we can enjoy beauty and kindness. If we are not skillful, we view life dismally. We feel hatred toward the person we love. Instead, we need to open the door of our hearts in the direction of happiness. Don't open the door in the direction of sorrow and unhappiness.

For example, let's say we look at other people around us with suspicion. That doesn't hurt them at all, it hurts us. If we open our hearts to love and compassion and learn to look at life with the eyes of a child, without preconceived notions, then we establish happiness. Then no material gifts in the world can be equal to or surpass the value of that experience of happiness. We must cultivate happiness by the way we look at things. If we open the doors of our hearts, then we can find happiness.

I try this exercise each morning: I say to myself, "Today might be the last day I view these lights of the city. Maybe I won't be able to do this tomorrow." When my mind has sadness, restlessness, or anger, then this reminder helps me to cultivate happiness and compassion, and to make my life bloom as a flower. We can't buy it; it is already present in our hearts.

Next, if we have the opportunity to observe nature, we can learn many lessons. The first lesson is the relaxation and letting go in nature. For example, in the plant kingdom, when autumn comes, the leaves fall from the tree naturally. Elephants leave their herd when they are about to die. We don't know where they go. Whales too go off alone to die. People cannot even find the skeletons of whales that have died in the ocean. Nobody has been able to find their graves. There has never been a plant or an animal whose mind is burdened like a human mind. Animals don't build gravesites. Humans want to be remembered and known forever. Our mind is so dear to us. All our joys, sorrows, anger, and love, we store these all in our consciousness carefully. And for what? Not to enrich ourselves. So we can learn from our mistakes? Not true. Each unskillfulness is different. Each day is a new day. Each breath is a new breath. Nothing repeats itself. No species retains its own characteristics as it evolves. No plant stays the same. Life changes. So storing up all the things we call past joy, past happiness, is the wrong way to live. We hold onto them like treasures. We want to invite our joys back into our memory to spice up our lives. But we also store our anger, sorrow, and hatred. Let us look at which of these we remember more often. It is the anger and the sorrow. When our love is young we think, "How can I live without my beloved one?" Later in life we think, "I don't want to see this person's face again for a hundred years."

We have never learned our lesson of letting go. Our lives are heavy with anger, sorrow, and jealousy because we store so much of them, and they are rushing around in our minds all the time. Our past joys and sorrows are not visible. We cannot measure them, but they have a lot of weight. They weigh our consciousness down, and we try to dream, to plan our futures with our hopes. But we don't see that by projecting from our past experiences, nothing can be different in our future experiences. For example, if we have a lot of misfortunes, we dream of a realm in the future where we'll be reborn in a sweet and beautiful Buddha Land. But in our lives, if we are not able to touch that in the present, what hope is there that it will be any different in the next life, in the Pure Land, in paradise?

If we have happiness and joy now in the present, then we can transform our past into something happy. Then we don't need to be weighed down by the past. So how exactly is it that when we live happily and joyfully in the present moment we can fix the past and enrich our future? On a shallow level, the answer is that when you don't have joy or happiness, when life is empty, then we invite things in from the past to fill up our minds, and we project that into our future. If we are happy now, we don't have to think about tomorrow. For example, a rich person who has abundance doesn't have to worry about the past or the future. It is the same in our spiritual life. If we have enough joy and happiness in the present, we don't have to invite the past up and worry about our happiness in the future.

If you have happy moments in the present, then your past is full of these beautiful moments from the present as they move into the past. Life is only available here and now, and then the future is nourished by the beautiful moments of the past, which are the present moments which become the past. Our wholesome mental formations are nourished and strengthened by these beautiful moments in the present and the unwholesome mental formations lose their strength as we move into the future. Let us acknowledge all the conditions of happiness that are present today. Let us recognize them so we don't allow them to pass us by. Let us be able to feel nature and the love from our friends and family. Let us open our hearts and the doors of our hearts. Let us open the right compartments of our hearts. Don't invite up the sad memories from the past. Close those doors and let those memories drift away into oblivion. Let us take our lives into our own hands. Take this moment to practice mindfulness. Use this present moment. If you don't, you'll lose the present, the past and the future.

Here is a story. A Zen student asks his master, "What is the path of practice to calm my mind?" The Zen master instructs his student, "Tell me one sentence." The teacher says, "Come over here. Tell me." The student comes over, and then the master scolds him, "You don't have the capacity to listen to me yet. You just follow me. You don't have the capacity to stop in this present moment." Later the student asks again, "Please tell me the path of practice to calm my mind." The Zen master again says, "Come over here." But this time the student does not come, and the master scolds him again, "I told you to come over here and you don't listen to me. Get out!"

What is the meaning of this story? We all know that the purpose of living in the present moment is to enrich our lives and cut down the emotions from the past. We don't have to search for anything. While walking, eating, or listening to the sound of the bell, we just bring our mind back to the body. It's that simple. Of course, it's difficult for the mind to stay in the present moment. Zen masters in the old days had special ways of showing this teaching to their students.

If we live with this teaching, then we eliminate those emotions. Our minds shouldn't run into the past or the future. Being able to not let our mind wander means to stop right here: on this cup of water [pointing to a cup of water] or on this step. The mind is present with each word.

Here is another story. A man comes to a monastery to learn the practice from a Zen master. When he arrives, the Zen master asks him, "Have you had your tea yet?" and the new student answers, "Yes." So the teacher instructs him, "Go to the kitchen to eat your meal." Another new student is standing nearby, and the Zen master asks him, "Have you been here before?" and the student answers, "No." So the Zen master instructs him, "Go drink your tea." When the students leave, the monastic attendant of the Zen master asks him, "What is the purpose of these teachings?" To which the Zen master replies, "Drink your tea." All the master is doing is helping us to bring our mind to the present moment. That's all, to allow our mind to shine, which is what happens when we dwell in the present moment. Everything has a cycle. We are not this body. We are not the whispering voice. We are the stream of life. We are able to move into the flow of nature. Our body is just a shell. Our emotions, our thinking are just a shell. The only thing that stays with us is the recognition. This is eternal life in us. Have faith in it.

Here's an example: When it is very cold outside, we put on a lot of layers of clothing to keep us warm. Then, when we come into the meditation hall where it is warmer than outside, we take some of those layers of clothing off. The layers can be compared to the five *skandas*. The outer layer, layer number one is the body. The emotions, layer number two, are not us. Sometimes we wear a coat of sadness. Sometimes we wear a coat of happiness. When our mind is calm, we are clear and alert. No one can take that away from us. When our mind is lost, then we are gone. Another layer is the coat of thinking. It is difficult for others to perceive our thinking. When you recognize you are thinking, just stop. Thinking is like a layer of clothing.

We are alive, and there is no greater joy. We can hang up our thinking and see, "This is my thinking. This is not me." We can wear the layers, or we can take them off. We are the owner that recognizes these things. We recognize thinking but do not identify with it. Then we can use this path to go into nirvana. People used to sit in meditation for twenty years and go through seven cushions before they could realize this. Let us recognize the stream of no-birth and no-death. We are so fortunate to encounter the dharma. Come back to yourself and recognize that you have the capacity to practice well.

CHAPTER ELEVEN
Quietude

When we listen to music, there are musical notes, but there are also silences within the music that are as essential as the notes themselves. Similarly in our lives, we require quiet times that bring more quietude to our lives.

This gift is the gift of quietude from the mountains. I ask you to bring that gift into your own heart, because the quietude is already inside of you. It is a gift you can carry with you wherever you go.

The most valuable gift is to be able to taste the enjoyment of your own life. You have to be intelligent and spiritual to cultivate the ability to enjoy what is already inside of you. If you can, then even in old age you can fill your daily life with joy, and then you become a gift to others.

Praise to Shakyamuni Buddha, the Fully Awakened One.

Respected community, today is quite a special day. It is the day when we celebrate Vu Lan, also called Ullambana. We also have come to call it the Rose for Your Pocket Ceremony. The invitation for this event said, "We will walk together. We will breathe together. We will smile together. We will listen to the dharma talk together. We will listen to the birds singing together." I was not there when the brothers and sisters prepared the flier, but if it were up to me I would have taken out the words "listen to the dharma talk." This doesn't mean the dharma talk is not important. But the gift of being here at Deer Park is not just in the dharma talk. The greatest gift the community has to offer you here is the space that is very peaceful and tranquil. Some of us came here yesterday and had the opportunity to stay overnight. The full moon last night was more beautiful here than in the city because we are at a higher altitude. In the early morning, the fog is beautiful, and we can only see the peaks of the mountains in a very vague way. The freshness of the monks and nuns, the quietude of space, the immense silence of the mountains is the greatest gift. That is why I think the dharma talk is a little bit extraneous. You need only experience this spaciousness. That is the greatest gift of this place.

I like to come to the meditation hall very early in the morning before the monks and nuns arrive for sitting meditation. I even came here early to sit before this dharma talk while the sangha was still outside enjoying walking meditation. I like to come here to enjoy this immense space in this lovely dharma hall. Each one of us could create a place like Deer Park ourselves if we worked hard for our whole lives, became millionaires, bought all these acres of land, etc. But if we are intelligent, we don't have to sweat or pay any money at all and this meditation hall is all ours. Then we can take advantage of all the challenges of our daily lives to deepen our practice.

Dear friends, we may think that we have to work hard for the rest of our lives. But if you came here for the bright moon, for the dew of fall, please stop and remember this quiet space exists both outside of us and inside of us. We are capable of singing like the children in Vietnam who memorize songs about the famous places that are dear to them in the regions where they grew up. I had a disciple whom I would ask to sing me the song of his childhood from the region where he was born. I remember a few lines from his song: "Wherever you go, remember the river and mountain, and all the famous names of the special places of our country."

The mountains of Deer Park offer you the bright moon. It is so quiet here in the morning. In the afternoon when it is quiet, we can take some time to write poetry. I am reminded of hearing the poetry of Dung Nham, the poem entitled "The Eye of the Person from the West Mountain." There is a line that goes, "You run from the world and battleground. We have gone through much suffering." This poem mentions the names of many places such as Bến Tre, the names of mountains and rivers, and the memory of these places touches something in our hearts and something real in our consciousness.

Some people have come to Deer Park this weekend for the first time. There are other people who come here often and have contributed to our community in many ways. All of us have a place reserved in our hearts for Deer Park, not necessarily for a particular monk or nun, because we monastics rotate to different practice centers every few years, but for the mountains and the space in the mountains which are constant.

The most precious gift this practice center has to offer is the quietude and the tranquility of these mountains. As monks and nuns, we may not be very young or beautiful, but this monastic life is one of freshness. I spend a lot of time in the city, and whenever I return to Deer Park, I feel I am coming home. I feel I am a fish put back in a pond again. I feel I can breathe again.

The first gift this center offers you is the peace, quietude, and tranquility of this place. We need this in our lives which can become so hectic and stressful in the cities.

Dear community, in our lives we need quietude so very much. We need moments of it, and this is very important. When we listen to music, there are musical notes, but there are also silences within the music that are as essential as the notes themselves. Similarly in our lives, we require quiet times that bring more quietude to our lives. Those who are intelligent bring quietude back to their minds whenever possible. There are two kinds of quietude that we can experience in our consciousness. Sometimes we can feel suffocated and feel a burning heat when it is quiet. It can be quiet but very heavy, not happy, struggling, with a weight on our consciousness. Why is it we feel a burning inside? What happens that we cannot enjoy the quiet? It is because we have too many things in our minds that we cannot say. We have complexes of superiority, complexes of inferiority, complexes of equality, and we cannot find a way to express all the complexities in our minds. With certainty, this kind of energy could explode the whole planet.

We need to be able to recognize and differentiate between the quietude of happiness and the silence of enduring, of implosion or of explosion. That second kind of energy can create a big knot inside of us that destroys our bodies and minds, that turns into tumors and illness. There are certain silences that we need to resolve and let go.

There is a mother who asked her son, "Do you know what we have shoulders for?" Her son wasn't really sure and said, "To hold your head up." She said to him, "No, you don't understand the meaning of life yet." So the son thought about it, and one day he saw some people carrying things and realized that might be the answer. So he went to his mother and answered, "To carry heavy weights." She said, "That is almost correct, but not quite right." Shortly after that, the son's father passed away. The suffering of the mother was too great for her to bear, so her friend said to her, "You can lean on my shoulder to cry on." Then the son understood. The necessity of shoulders is for others to lean on and to cry on.

We can wash away the painful silences of our lives with the drops of our tears. We need to cry to resolve the blocks of suffering and injustices in us. When there is suffering, it can tear our insides apart, and when it releases, we can become much lighter. When we share it with somebody, our suffering has wings and flies high. When our suffering becomes too great, people cannot bear it and don't know how to resolve it. We need to pay attention to our suffering. We need to share it with somebody and allow the tears to clear our hearts and to purify the suffering that many generations, not only ourselves, have had to bear so that the suffering can lessen. Our strength is not just in this body. Our strength also lies in our loved ones, in our children, and in our friends. We need to help them to understand us. We need to use their shoulders so that we can release our suffering. If there are afflictions in your heart, you can let yourself cry, and you can share it with your children and spouse. You can empty your heart and heal your body and mind of the blocks which can form tumors. We have the capacity to destroy or cure our own lives.

Dear friends, in Vietnamese culture, this day of Ullambana is called the Day of Gratitude, and for the last twenty years or so we have also called it the Rose for Your Pocket. We recognize the gratitude we have for our parents and also we have the opportunity for cleansing our own blocks of suffering, the things hidden in our own hearts, sometimes hidden even from ourselves.

There is a story that is very famous in Vietnam about a princess and a boatman. This is a lovely story. It is sad, but it reflects the truth that a teardrop can release great suffering. There is a boatman who is very ugly, so during the day he hides himself so that no one will see his face. In the evening, he comes out and plays the flute. He is very poor and takes care of a boat, and while he is out in the boat, he sings about his own life. He plays the flute very beautifully, and the sound of the flute travels to the palace of a beautiful young lady who falls in love with him because of the beautiful sound of his flute. We call this type of love *mê* in Vietnamese which means infatuation. This kind of infatuation can be dangerous because it can break someone's heart or twist someone's mind. So the beautiful sound of the flute of the young man traveled into the room of the princess and she fell in love with the man. She couldn't eat or sleep and became very ill. The family became very concerned about her health and wanted to help her. They figured out what had happened and invited the man to play the flute in her room because they thought that perhaps this could help her to become well. This boatman was very poor and very ugly. He was ashamed to show his face, but he agreed to come and play the flute in order to help the princess on one condition. He said, "The one condition is she cannot look at my face." The princess agreed, and he began to play the flute. But her heart ripened with love at the sound of the flute. She said, "I don't care how ugly you are, I must look at you, and then I could die." So she took one look at him, and she screamed and fainted.

After seeing his face, the princess was not infatuated with the boatman anymore. However he fell deeply in love with her. This was an infectious love. Now he became ill. He could not play the flute anymore. He became sick, and within a month or so he died. This was a very deep infatuation. It was very pitiful that the boatman didn't have any money or relatives to care for him. He just died and was buried by the side of the road. After a while his grave was upturned, and the people found that his heart had hardened. They could knock on it and it was like a diamond, or like marble. So the people carved it into a teacup. When there was tea in that cup, one could hear the sound of the flute and see the boat of the boatman in that cup of tea.

The father of the princess heard this story and asked to buy the teacup. Then when his daughter learned about it, she asked to see this teacup. Sure enough, they poured tea into it and they could see the boat and hear the sound of the flute. This princess recognized that this was the same sound of the flute that she used to listen to, and she felt full of regret and pain for the suffering of the boatman. In that moment, the princess recognized the deep suffering of the boatman. She began to cry, and her tears fell into the cup of tea. Somehow the boatman felt her compassion, and he no longer suffered. He felt her care for him and was deeply touched by that, and in that moment the teacup shattered into pieces. The lesson of this story is that there are sufferings that can be washed away by drops of tears.

I don't know if you have experienced anything like this. I know I have. When I was younger and my mother scolded me, I wasn't afraid. But when we sat down together and she began to cry, her tears were the most frightening thing to me. Those tears could wash away a lot of suffering and injustices that we might have caused each other. Of course, we are very unskillful. We have blocks of suffering we store up. If we are intelligent, we need to learn to practice to take care of the suffering right away so it doesn't accumulate.

For example, certain cuts heal quickly, but other times we are left with a scar. Sometimes we can violate somebody, and it is very difficult to remove the offending words from the other person's consciousness. We have to practice to calm our minds, to lighten our minds, to allow our minds to soar.

We need silences in our lives to cultivate quietude, fulfillment, and happiness. There are silences within us full of war and hatred that are heavy and suffocating. If we cannot clearly distinguish the different faces of these silences, we will not be able to do much with our lives.

How can we truly taste the flavor of silence and the undisturbed mind? How can we be happy? Once we have a taste of these experiences, we realize that they can dissolve all knots within our consciousness and cleanse our hearts until there is no trace of sadness, sorrow, or suffering. If you can learn to look deeply into your own mind, you can see that there are burning areas, spaces that are very busy. But there are also spaces that are very quiet. If we are intelligent and careful, we can see moments full of hate, loss, aversion, and grasping. But there are also pauses in our mind, like the pauses in a piece of music between the notes. Looking deeply, we can see that there are many conditions that bring about these moments of pause. Often we don't recognize when they are present, and therefore don't know how to cultivate them.

In Zen, we call these moments of pause by many different names: mindfulness, seeing our true face, seeing our true nature, seeing our true self. In order to cultivate these moments, it requires passion and dedication to stop and bring peace and quietude into our minds. If you have enough awareness of your own life, you will do anything to cultivate these moments, because you realize that these moments are the greatest gift.

The Sutra Agama has a line in it that speaks to this. There was an old woman in the city of Vesali. She hated the Buddha and vowed that she would never meet him. One day while she was walking, the Buddha appeared to be walking toward her. So she turned in the other direction. But as soon as she did, the Buddha appeared there too. So she turned in another direction, and the Buddha appeared there too. Whatever direction she turned in, he was there. She became so angry that she decided to stand there and cover her eyes with her hands. She thought that the Buddha would eventually get tired of waiting there and would go away. She did not think he would be patient enough to stand there all day. So she waited.

It is not certain whether this story really happened, but it gives us a suggestion. All we need to do is to peek through our fingers, and we will see the Buddha very clearly.

If we are intelligent, we can ask, "What does it mean that the Buddha is present in that pause?" There is a certain bitterness that puts a heavy weight on our hearts and minds. The only way to resolve that bitterness is to recognize its presence. We recognize, "This is my sadness, this is my anger, this is a part of me, but it is not mine." This sounds theoretical, but everything the Buddha taught is based on this foundation. This body is yours, but this body is not you. If you think it is you, then you throw yourself into your sadness and let it drown you. If you are intelligent, then you can recognize, "A sadness is passing through my mind right now." The sadness has birth and death. It arises and it ceases. We are something that can observe it. We can recognize it. If we are not skillful, we see things come and go, but we do not see the quietude. If we are skillful, we see the moment when there is no sadness, no grasping. Then we can widen that gap. This is not the silence of heaviness. It is the silence full of joy, understanding and mindfulness. When we widen and deepen the silence, it improves the quality of our lives.

For example, many of us came to America from Vietnam. The English language is very different from the Vietnamese language. The Vietnamese and Chinese languages are monosyllabic, but the English language is not. Initially when we hear people speaking in English, it sounds like they are speaking non-stop without any break between the words because we don't recognize the language. But when we get used to hearing English, we begin to hear the spaces between the words. We can discern the pauses. It is just like this when we listen to music. After some practice, we can begin to discern the different instruments, like the drum and the flute. When we look at our minds, we see that there are certain wide spaces in our consciousness. Then we can practice to recognize those spaces and to widen them so that we can prolong them. We don't have to *do* anything. We can just enjoy the quietude.

In conclusion, there are different kinds of valuable gifts. There are the expensive gifts that cost a lot of money. We have to work hard to earn the money to buy these gifts so that we can carry them home. Deer Park cannot offer expensive gifts like these. What we *can* offer you is right here. This gift is the gift of quietude from the mountains. I ask you to bring that gift into your own hearts, because that quietude is already inside of you. It is a gift you can carry with you wherever you go.

As people, we can earn money from our labor and enjoy that. We can enjoy nature, like looking at the sky and the earth or taking time to enjoy watching the ants pass by. You can enjoy all of these things. But the most valuable gift is to be able to taste the enjoyment of your own life. You have to be intelligent and spiritual to cultivate the ability to enjoy what is already inside of you. If you can, then even in old age you can fill your daily life with joy, and then you become a gift to others. If we can't do this and the quality of the life inside of us is not high, then we cannot do anything to serve anyone.

What is most important and valuable is to bring this quietude into our own minds and hearts. You can begin anew today with this Ullambana ceremony. If we are full of misery, let us take refuge in each other to cleanse the knots in our own lives. This ceremony is very meaningful, and I am glad that you have this wonderful opportunity to benefit from it today.

APPENDICES

KH'OB

APPENDIX ONE
Biography of Thầy Giác Thanh
by Venerable Thích Phước Tịnh
(Translated from Vietnamese text by Chân Hão and
Chân Tuệ Năng. Some minor changes and additions
have been made for the English version.)

Thầy Giác Thanh was also known as Dạ Hạc,
Venerable Tâm Tông, Chân Giác Thanh, pen name
Trạm Nhiên, birth name Lê Văn Hiếu.

Thầy Giác Thanh was born on June 9, 1947, in a
quiet and remote hamlet of Trà Lộc, in Sóc Sơn
Village, Tri Tôn District, Rạch Giá Province. His
father was Lê Văn Đạt, and his mother was Nguyễn
Thi Nhớ. He was the third child in the family of
four sons and two daughters.

Like many other children in the countryside of
Vietnam growing up in the great suffering of their
country caused by wars and poverty, Thầy Giác
Thanh had to learn at an early age to follow his
older brothers and sisters to gather food and catch
fish. From this, his elegant face became golden-
tanned by the tropical sunlight. In spite of his
hardships, the seed of compassion had been present
within him, perhaps for many lifetimes. At the early
age of seven or eight, he shed tears when thinking
of our small human life in the vastness of infinite
existence. Thầy's stay in this little village ended
when his parents moved to Rạch Giá City. While in
the city he began learning to write his first alphabet.
During this time there were some relatively
peaceful periods without bombings and fighting
because of the Geneva Peace Accord.

As time passed, the little boy with the golden-tanned face from the remote hamlet of Trà Lộc became one of the best students of Nguyễn Trung Trực School, very intelligent and especially very brave. Perhaps he had inherited his bravery from patriot Nguyễn Trung Trực. Thầy Giác Thanh expressed love for his country in his first poem *Tears for My Homeland,* written when he was in grade twelve, 1967:

> *Oh my beloved homeland,*
> *So many long quiet nights*
> *I lay awake, crying tears of love for you.*
> *Oh my beloved homeland,*
> *What have you done to deserve this?*
> *To let those demons torture you so,*
> *Without remorse, compassion, or brotherly*
> *love.*
> *They sold you to the Devil King.*
> *Out of love for you*
> *I buy you back with my own flesh and blood,*
> *With my wisdom, my very heart,*
> *And with my whole being.*
> *Even if this body burns into ashes,*
> *I vow to spread them along the road to*
> *peace.*

There is a saying, "Man should have determination to penetrate the deep skies." If one does not want to be a speck of dust blown away by a whirlwind destroying one's own country, then one should not participate in the destruction. Better, one should be a lone traveler on the path of no-birth and no-death. Thầy Giác Thanh turned his life toward cultivating his ideal of great compassion and liberation through inner discovery. In 1967 he became a novice monk

at Thành Hoa Temple, Tấn Mỹ Village, Chợ Mới
District, Long Xuyên Province. His Dharma name,
Giác Thanh (Awakening Sound), was given to him
by his teacher, Venerable Phổ Huệ.

He stayed in Giác Nguyên Temple (Sài Gòn) in
1968, and then in Xá Lợi Temple in 1969. He was
fully ordained in Giác Viên Temple in the autumn
of 1970. In 1971 he attended the University of Vạn
Hạnh to further his studies in Buddhism. He never
stopped searching; whenever there was a talk by a
well-known teacher he would be there. Then he
received further inspiration on his path when he
came across the book of guidance for the monastic
life practiced at the True Emptiness Monastery.
Although he was not a permanent resident of the
monastery, he participated in every summer Rains
Retreat.

In the spring of 1974 he returned to the True
Emptiness Monastery, entering its second four-year
program. The days passed, listening to the sutras in
the morning, meditating in the afternoon, drinking
tea, looking at dewdrops hanging from the leafy
roof, and watching the rays of sunlight shining and
merging with the firelight in the hearth. The love
from his brothers and the teachings of his old
teacher on the peak of Tao Phung Mountain opened
his heart and lit up the path to the true nature for
this young destitute. Thầy Giác Thanh was a very
good meditator and one of the most beloved elder
brothers at True Emptiness Monastery. Those who
had a chance to know him had beautiful memories
of him. He offered love, tenderness, and support to
lay practitioners as well as his newly ordained
brothers and sisters. With his deep understanding

and compassion he created great harmony in the sangha.

Once again, Vietnam's history turned to a new page. After the spring of 1975 (when the communists took over the whole country), the peaceful years at True Emptiness Monastery faded into the past. Everybody now had to work hard in the fields under the hot, burning sun. While working, Thầy sometimes stopped and asked the question, "One's awakening is not yet realized, why should one waste one's precious life to gain some food? My dear younger brothers and sisters, we should give ourselves time for reflection." Whenever there was an opportunity, he would contemplate with his little tea set beside the bamboo grove in the front yard. Often at dawn and dusk, seeing the floating mist, he also felt the human love floating and fading away. He wrote:

> *Existing in this life,*
> *I know how to enjoy tea alone.*
> *Thirty years, a dream gone by,*
> *Day and night, the little pot of tea is my only*
> *friend.*

In the winter of 1977 he left Thường Chiếu Monastery and built Ẩn Không hut in Mỹ Lường Village. This hut was made with bamboo leaves. Next to the hut was his small meditation space. The setting expressed the meditative state of a Zen master with a simple and noble life, but it also expressed the artistry of a poet. After four years he left Ẩn Không hut as described in the last paragraph of the poem, *A Yellow Flower Dream:*

I am a traveler
In infinite time.
My soul seems to get lost in the desolate
island.
One morning, the island awakens,
Birds shouting, rushing me onto my path.
And in the vast billowy ocean,
The dust of life is washed off.

In July of 1981 he escaped Vietnam by boat, crossing the Thailand Bay. Like many other Vietnamese people enduring dangerous escapes, he was not able to avoid pirates. Seeing the cruel raping of women and grabbing of jewelry, angrily he asked, "Do you have a heart? How could you be so cruel to your fellow humans?" The pirates were angry and threw him into the ocean. Fortunately, the head pirate, in a flash of sympathy, tossed him a rope and pulled him up onto the boat. So the game of birth and death was once more postponed.

Thầy was in Song La refugee camp in Indonesia from July 1981 to early 1982. He was sponsored by Venerable Thích Mãn Giác to come to Los Angeles. He spent his first refugee allowance of $300 to buy an expensive antique tea set and some tea and offered the first cup of tea to the Venerable Thích Mãn Giác. What was the cost of a cup of tea? A small expense, but this action expressed the gratitude of a young wandering man. The Venerable offered a cooling shade and a loving harbor for Thầy Giác Thanh. During Thầy's brief stay at Phật Giáo Vietnam Temple, the Venerable, like a tender and caring mother, offered the loving energy that healed the wounds in the wanderer's heart. At the end of spring 1982, at the request of the Venerable

Thích Mãn Giác, Thầy moved to Nam Tuyên Temple in Virginia to help Thầy Trí Tuệ. They lived happily together from 1982 to 1989.

During that time, Thầy Giác Thanh also lived and practiced in Japanese, Korean, and Burmese practice centers. The appeal of a traveler's life faded, however, as his journey of coming home was still burning deep within him. Continuously he searched, knocking at different great teachers' doors, for the final breakthrough to penetrate directly into infinite space.

In one of the North American retreats led by Thầy Nhất Hạnh at the end of summer 1986, seeing Thầy Giác Thanh practice with intense and strained effort, Thầy Nhất Hạnh said to him, "Thầy Giác Thanh, you do not need to strive so much. Walk with me and look at the beautiful autumn leaves changing colors from yellow to red. Life is such a miracle; it is never born and never dies. Look deeply and accept life as it is." These teaching words of Thầy Nhất Hạnh were like a few drops of water causing a full cup to overflow, like lightning penetrating deep layers of clouds and illuminating the immense sky. Since then, he stopped the search through strained effort.

In the summer retreat of 1990 at Plum Village, the retreatants had a chance to practice with a Vietnamese monk, Thầy Giác Thanh, one with a peaceful smile that expressed his inner peace. In 1991 he began residing at Plum Village, and there he lived happily with his teacher, Thầy Nhất Hạnh, the old oak tree, and he himself [Thầy Giác Thanh] became an oak tree protecting his younger brothers

and sisters, young oak trees. He also led Days of
Mindfulness at the Cactus Meditation Center
located near Paris, France. He was called by a very
poetic name, Thầy Cactus. He was given this name
because he looked after the Cactus Meditation
Center, but it was an appropriate name for his
permeating but gentle radiance and upright manner.
At the end of 1991 he received the Lamp
Transmission to become a Dharma Teacher and a
gatha from Thầy Nhất Hạnh. The gatha is:

> *The awakened nature is the true nature.*
> *Pure sound is the manifestation of the*
> *Wonderful Sound.*
> *The full moon light illuminates Tỳ Lô Ocean.*
> *The musical waves are still strong and*
> *sonorous.*

And this is Thầy Giác Thanh's insight gatha offered
to his teacher and the sangha at his Lamp
Transmission:

> *Clear water on one side,*
> *Urine on the other,*
> *All will return to sky, clouds, oceans and*
> *rivers.*
> *There is sunlight during daytime*
> *And moonlight at night*
> *Shining my way.*

For Thầy Giác Thanh, Plum Village was a cradle in
which all of humankind's happiness could flourish
and a field in which the seeds of compassion and
understanding could be sown. He wrote a poem to
express his respect and admiration for his teacher:

A lightning look
Brings down several great walls.
I bow my head to receive
And remember it life after life.

Thầy Nhất Hạnh offered him a small wooden hut on the forest edge beside his own. All year round one could hear birds singing and see many different flowers blooming around his hut. He liked the name Floating Cloud. There was a vast space in his heart. He walked freely and solidly, and his smiles and words carried profound peace to people around him. Therefore, in 1992, in his very first visit to the East Coast of North America, he brought a lot of happiness to the practitioners participating in the various retreats and Days of Mindfulness that he led. One thing was sure wherever he went—France, America, Australia, Canada—from the beginning of his teaching to his last breath, all of us received his tender, fresh, and peaceful energy. He was respected and deeply loved by us all.

In 1995 he contracted tuberculosis, and his diabetes worsened. He had lived with his illness since 1992 or earlier. With his mindful breathing, he embraced his illnesses. He took care of his illnesses like a mother loving her child, never complaining no matter how demanding the child was. Many of our ancestors also faced challenging obstacles but took them as opportunities to realize full enlightenment. Similarly, even with these serious illnesses, Thầy could live peacefully and happily, and this was clearly expressed in his poems, especially those written after 1997, such as *Mind Seal*:

Stepping on the land of reality

Fresh, beautiful flowers bloom everywhere.
Only deep mindfulness shines through
And the three realms have been surpassed...

Or *Light of Winter*, which is like a strong
proclamation:

Facing white snow
Suddenly,
One-self fading away
The whole universe
Turning into a great lamp.

In 1997 Thầy Giác Thanh became the Head of
Practice at the Maple Forest Monastery at the Green
Mountain Dharma Center in Vermont. He offered a
stable and joyful presence for the young brothers,
sisters, and lay practitioners there. A few years
later, in early 2000, some of the Plum Village
Sangha members began looking for property to start
a West Coast monastery. Acquiring the land for
Deer Park Monastery and then becoming the abbot
of the monastery, Thầy Giác Thanh knew that this
place would be the last one of his life. Therefore, he
used all of his remaining strength to build this place
in showing his gratitude to his most respected
teacher. His illnesses became seriously life-
threatening, and finally, like the cycles of birth and
death of all phenomena, he returned his
impermanent body to the Mother Earth. As the
arahats said upon entering nirvana, "The most
important task has been completed." Thầy Giác
Thanh arrived in Deer Park in the summer of 2000
and left us in the autumn of 2001. His stay in Deer
Park was very short compared to an average human
lifespan, and nothing compared to the age of the

stars and moons, but his accomplishment is great
and has entered into our hearts. A kind, gentle, and
loving voice, a joyful smile until the end of his life,
a deep and clear wisdom, great compassion, and
peaceful steps, all revealed his profound
understanding of no coming, no going. That is the
greatest gift he has offered to his brothers and
sisters and to the sanghas all over the world.

Thầy is truly a Dharma Teacher of many Western
and Vietnamese practitioners. Although he passed
away, he has transformed to be one with us. His
words are like essential keys to open the door to
one's wisdom, happiness, and compassion,
especially his last dharma talks in the Full Moon
meditation hall. How deep his words are! He is the
most loved elder brother. Each one of us remembers
him in our own way. He is a brother, protective,
sometimes strict. He is a mother, loving and taking
care of us. He is a friend, opening his heart to us.
He loved his brothers and sisters wholeheartedly.
He is a meadow, full of exotic, simple, and beautiful
flowers and grass, in which each one of us can play
freely. Being with him, we see ourselves
disappearing and merging with him, like a river
merging into the ocean. We all think it is very
difficult to find another elder brother like him. Here
are a few lines from a poem written for his younger
brothers and sisters:

> *...Please do not scold or blame*
> *My younger brothers and sisters*
> *For I fear that the gray color of sadness*
> *Would darken their pure hearts.*

Thầy Giác Thanh was also a student with deep gratitude. He respected wholeheartedly Thầy Nhất Hạnh and other teachers. He always did his best to help spread the teachings, even when he was very sick. In October 2000, when his former teacher Venerable Thanh Từ visited the United States, Thầy and some monks, nuns, and lay friends successfully and humbly coordinated the public talks for him in Southern California.

On his return to Vietnam in 1992, his old friends were very surprised by his simplicity. They could not believe that he had experienced great suffering, disappointments, many ups and downs, profound transformations, and attained great wisdom and understanding of the dharma from inspiring teachers. Wearing the brown [Order of] Interbeing jacket and carrying his monastic shoulder bag, he traveled humbly without formal welcoming or farewells. With his gentle smiles, he overcame all the political obstacles he encountered while in Vietnam and therefore was able to successfully offer the Dharma and charity to many people there. Although he had a busy schedule, he still spent time with his relatives and old friends, monastic and non-monastic. He treated them with love from his whole heart. When they saw him again, they were deeply moved to tears. Before coming back to the United States, he searched for and bought a special tea set as a gift for his closest friend. Not many of his friends were able to be with him in the hospital or attend his funeral, but the deep caring and love from those who were present revealed how much love he had given us.

In his second return to Vietnam in 1999, he told his friends, "I came back to visit all of you for the last time. I don't think that I will be able to make another trip." His words seemed like a joke and nobody could believe what he said would be true. In this trip, one of his childhood friends helped him to fulfill his long-standing wish to help his family.

He lived humbly, freely, and with dignity. So beautifully he came and left. His life is like a pristine cactus flower blooming at night.

Close to death, he seemed to dwell more in the other realm, but when Thầy Nhất Hạnh spoke with him from Beijing the day before he died, he smiled and his face lit up. He opened his eyes to receive his teacher's words. Thầy Nhất Hạnh read the poem he had just written in honor of Thầy Giác Thanh:

> *That you are a real gentleman is known by everyone*
> *The work of a true practitioner has been accomplished*
> *When your stupa has just been raised on the hillside*
> *The sound of children's laughter will already be heard*

Later he added these two lines:

> *One maple leaf has fallen down and yet you continue to climb the hill of the twenty-first century with us.*
> *Thousands of daffodils are beginning to bloom and the Earth continues to be with the*

sky singing the song of no-birth and no-death.

Our ancestors said that once the most important task in life has been completed, one no longer needs to return to this world. However, great beings come and go freely to continue the bodhisattva's work. Dear Thầy Giác Thanh, we vow to be your companions on this path of love and liberation, life after life.

Deer Park Monastery in the Great Hidden Mountain
October 19, 2001
Venerable Thích Phước Tịnh

APPENDIX TWO
Letter to Mr. and Mrs. Hilsberg
(Translated from Vietnamese text by Vân Khánh Hà)

Deer Park Monastery, 20 February 2005

Dear Mr. and Mrs. Hilsberg,

I am very happy to write this letter with warm wishes and regards and to share my experience of the practice with both of you.

During the Buddha's time, there was a layperson named Anathapindika. When he was really ill, the Buddha's disciples would come and visit him and teach him about the practice.

Anathapindika practiced when he was seriously ill. His breathing was irregular, but within a short period of time of practicing he found peace and insight. His wisdom eye was opened, and he could taste liberation (nirvana). He left his body lightly just like someone leaving old and worn out shoes.

This is the practice:

> *Breathing in, I know I am breathing in.*
> *Breathing out, I know I am breathing out.*
>
> *Breathing in, I know that eyes, ears, nose, tongue, head, body, arms, and legs are not me.*

Breathing out, I know that eyes, ears, nose, tongue, head, body, arms, and legs are not me.

Breathing in, I know that happiness, sadness, worry, fear, and despair are not me.
Breathing out, I know that happiness, sadness, worry, fear, and despair are not me.

Breathing in, I know that all the never-ending thoughts are not me.
Breathing out, I know that all the never-ending thoughts are not me.

And from this practice, slowly we realize that I am not these objects of my observation. I am the observer. I am not the object being observed. I am the awareness. For example, illness is the illness of the body, and the awareness of the illness is not the body. The awareness of the illness is truly not the illness. This awareness is already within us. It is the awareness of "no-birth no-death." It is infinite life that is already within us.

For a long time we only think that we are the body. We are the feelings of happiness and sadness, we are the endless thoughts, and therefore we suffer. We have despair and fear. If you just return and become aware that we have the ability to recognize that those feelings are not us, if you have faith and believe in this, right away you can open the eye of wisdom and overcome a thousand sufferings, just like Anathapindika.

With little time and poor knowledge to express myself but with my sincere heart of a monk, I hope you both will practice diligently. You can read, "The Discourse on the Teachings to be Given to the Sick" (*Plum Village Chanting and Recitation Book*, page 267) so you can practice this more deeply.

I pray with the loving energy of all buddhas and bodhisattvas that they will protect and help you to overcome all your difficulties and find wisdom and insight.

Venerable Thích Phước Tịnh

APPENDIX THREE
Question and Answer with Venerable Thầy Phước Tịnh
(First published in the *Deer Park Breeze*, Spring 2003)

Venerable Thầy Phước Tịnh, Pure Merit, is a Dharma Teacher at the Quan Âm Temple in Đa Lạt, Việt Nam. He visited Plum Village in 2001, and in 2002, he joined the Plum Village Sangha. We are very fortunate to have him at Deer Park this year.

What is it like to be here at Deer Park? How is it different from temple life in Vietnam?

Generally speaking, there is no big difference between this Vietnamese-Western Sangha and any Sangha in Vietnam. The only differences are that here we have many different cultures, levels of education, and a wide range of ages, and we all come together to receive the same teachings from Thây [Thích Nhất Hạnh]. We should be strong and stable enough to help our younger brothers and sisters so that there is not much of a gap between older and younger monastics in terms of our practice and basic knowledge of the Buddha's teachings.

What do you feel Deer Park needs?

In any Sangha, wherever it is, the center of attention should be in developing and maintaining its strength: the bond between Sangha members, the harmony in the Sangha, the practice of the Sangha.

A Sangha which lacks these things is not a strong Sangha.

What do you want to offer Deer Park?

I would like to offer Deer Park my being here with the Sangha, practicing and sharing with the Sangha, according to my capacity.

A practice center is a place of practice. All of us come here to practice, not to gain power or to be "somebody." We should put our efforts into purifying our deluded mind, on helping each other, monastic as well as lay. It does not matter which tradition this practice center comes from. If we think that this is a Vietnamese, or Japanese, or Tibetan center, then we are not able to allow Buddhism to take root in the West. It does not matter which nationality our teacher is as long as we do our part to put the teachings into practice. Then the chance to develop strong Western Buddhism is very high. The stronger our practice, the faster the tree of Buddhism can grow and bear fruit.

Where do you get so much energy? [Thầy Phước Tịnh gives dharma talks twice a week and teaches three classes a week to the Sangha in addition to many consultations.]

My energy is from the Sangha's energy and vice-versa. If everyone is aware of this truth, then we can do a lot of things tirelessly and happily for ourselves and the Sangha in a relaxing and selfless way. I am just an ordinary monk. All I have to do every day is to keep my practice constant and steady and to do wholeheartedly whatever community work is assigned to me. If everyone is doing his or her part without reserve, then the energy of the Sangha will be tremendous, and everyone will benefit from this energy. We do not have to be the best in organizing a retreat, in giving a Dharma talk, etc.; all we have to be is consistent and diligent. If the motivation behind our work is to receive recognition, then no matter how good our work, we are expecting something in return and cannot be happy and at peace.

APPENDIX FOUR
Tea with the Venerable, Part I
(September 2005)

*In a discussion on the topic of my project to write
this book (Be Like a Tree), the Venerable shared
with me and other practitioners about his
understanding of Chinese Zen. He explained that
Chinese Zen has a rich tradition in the Chinese
culture that is over a thousand years old. They used
koans, however these koans have been very difficult
for Westerners to access because, for one thing,
many of them have been translated from Chinese to
Vietnamese to English. He then shared two ways to
enhance our spiritual life.*

The first way is to take it slowly and go from the
outside to the inside. We can deal with what is
inside of us by observing what is outside of us and
move from the outside in. This is called *shamanta*
or stopping. We take the form of the practice and
only later apply it to our inner world. The second
way to practice is from the inside out. We take the
heart of the true practice and only then do we move
to the outside. This is the Chinese way and can also
be called insight meditation. However, the Chinese
Zen practice of insight meditation is different from
and harder than the American understanding of
insight meditation. This is because the language of
the Chinese Zen masters is hard to decipher. It is a
secretive language and is like a puzzle.

Here is an example of one such Zen story. A Zen
master asks his disciple, "What do we do whenever
a thief comes into our house and steals some things

but does not take all of our treasures?" The Zen student replies, "Why doesn't the thief take all of the treasures?" The master replies, "Because he is your friend. Since he is your friend, he won't take all of your treasures." Then the student asks, "Why would my friend come into my house and rob me of my things?"

How can we understand this story? This is a story about the practice of mindfulness. Let me try to explain the deep meaning of it. When we practice and breathe so that we are practicing well, and our mind wanders, then we know that we are not present. This is what the Zen master means by the statement that, "The thief has robbed you." But the thief has not robbed us of all our treasures, because if we are still mindful enough to see that the mind has wandered, then we still possess our treasure of mindfulness. We are still able to recognize that the mind has wandered, so the thief has not taken all the treasures.

When we are dealing with our emotions, at times the thief does rob us of all our treasures. The thief steals our mindfulness, and then we identify with our emotions and believe that we *are* our feelings or our anger, for example. But why in the story does the Zen master describe the thief as our friend? Because there is a spy inside the house, someone on the inside who is looking out for us. In the past, we may have watered a lot of wholesome seeds in our store consciousness. And those wholesome seeds, like the seed of mindfulness, are still there to come to our help when the thief comes in to rob us. Then, with our mindfulness, we can name whatever comes up and begin to see that it is separate from us and not us. It is as if our feelings belong to us or we own them, but they are not us. On the outside, things may seem to belong to us, like our body. We can look at our body, but looking deeply we see that "This is my body but I do not own it." On a deeper level, we can say that our feelings also belong to us. But the best way to look at our feelings is as guests in our minds. The guests come and go. But we have to find the master of the house. Who is the master inside of us? Our job is to regain our sovereignty. This is the gift of Chinese Zen, this idea that we are not our thinking. We are not our emotions. We are not our happiness or our sadness. We are the masters of all these things. When we realize this, then we have a chance in this life.

The Sixth Patriarch Hui-Neng belongs to this school of Zen. His teachings are very beautiful, and he is the first part of the stream of the river to flow to us. His teachings are very deep, and I have offered twenty dharma talks on his teachings in Vietnamese. It is wrong thinking to believe that we have to gain more money or achieve higher peaks of responsibility. We think that money equates to happiness. But our pursuit of fame and money uses up a lot of our time in our life. If we put all that time into the acquisition of money, then we do not have time to take care of our treasure. For example, if we believe that raising our children properly is the most important thing in this life, then that is where we should put our time and energy. We should allocate our time to that which brings us happiness and joy.

A practitioner then asked the Venerable a question about how to work with a koan.

Working with koans is not the best method of practice. It is better for us to use mindfulness and recognition of what is going on as our practice. Play, be natural, have fun, enjoy. That is the best way to practice. Just play. That is the basis of our practice. Practice first to build a foundation upon which to be able to play. Do it in a way that is natural and in a way that your practice brings you happiness. That is the most successful way to practice.

The last question was about how his disciples are doing at the temple where he had been the abbot in Dalat, Vietnam.

If I had never come to America, then the students in Dalat would not have had the many opportunities that have recently come their way to mature and grow up.

APPENDIX FIVE
Tea with the Venerable, Part II
(July 2006)

Here is a story about the differences between the hummingbirds and the bees. Hummingbirds fly very fast and beat their wings hundreds of times per minute. They need a lot of nectar to sustain them, and they use that nectar for their movement. But the bees go from flower to flower to flower storing up nectar. They take it to the hive, and they invest it for the queen bee and others bees in the hive. They never partake of the honey that is made from their collections. We should be like the hummingbirds, enjoying the garden, being present and mindful, and not like the bees, always trying to store pollen for the future.

The Venerable then asked if we had any questions. The first question was about whether a practitioner should change jobs or careers so that her work feels more rewarding, meaningful and worthwhile.

With all the practice it all comes down to mindfulness, to have an open heart and love that flows openly. It all starts with mindfulness. For example, if you look at a flower and you are mindful and you don't have any whispering voice, then you can appreciate the true beauty of the flower. If you are in contact with people, and if you use a mind that is very clear and you don't have any opinion, then you have an innocent, fresh mind, and you can truly see the people and who they are. I have two things to share:

1) If you are in contact with anything, the first thing you have to know is that it is impermanent. It has to change.
2) Stop and appreciate how it is at that moment. Everything is fresh, new, real, pure.

Let me give an example: Look at children. They can be so nice, so well-behaved, and so happy. At other moments they can be so angry, disturbing, and nasty to you. Everything is changing. Allow them to be who they are. If you know how to stop and return to mindfulness, you can accept them and not heap expectations on them. Don't be sad and stop enjoying the moment. Enjoy who they are. Most of the teachings are based on this. Please apply this daily.

The next question was about how to maintain mindfulness in the face of sadness, frustration, and disappointment at the end of a romantic relationship.

The root of everything is this: you have to be solid first. If you think someone else will bring you happiness, you are very wrong. Another person cannot give you solidity. When you are not solid, other people are not solid. Both are weak and cannot lean on each other. Once you practice deeply, once you are fresh and solid, then you can meet someone else who is solid too. It is crucial to find happiness in oneself and not in other people.

Usually in life there is something you chase after and are looking for, but that thing comes and goes. It's not always there for you. But there is something that you are not chasing after, and it can just come to you and stay with you and bring you a deep and lasting happiness.

The next question was about the events of September 11th, 2001 and the destruction of the World Trade Center. The practitioner suggested that there may have been a conspiracy to destroy the Twin Towers on the part of the United States government.

In society, politics is full of so many lies. But it is not real. The news is not based on reality or on the truth. If you hear something about politics, it's not based on the truth. You have to be aware of that. Like in any country, the president is not the only one who makes the decisions. There are people behind the scenes who make many decisions about politics. And you have to realize something like war is not a decision by one person. The same is true when it comes to the fate of the whole country regarding not only a war but also some event like a flood or an earthquake.

As practitioners, we have to change on the inside first before we can expect society or the world to change. If we cannot change ourselves, we cannot expect the world to change. Whatever happens in war or peace, bad or good, we have to go not outward to do something about it, we have to go inward first. We have to find and create peace, to change ourselves first, and only then can we expect the world around us to change.

First of all, we should not absorb all the news from the outside. First we need to practice until we as practitioners are strong. Don't study what's happening in the world. That can stir us up. First we need to be at peace. You need to find solidity in yourself first. Once you practice deeply and find yourself at peace, you will see what is happening in politics clearly and think about it with a lot of wisdom and insight.

The next question was from a practitioner who experiences severe asthma and has difficulties following her breath and relaxing with her breath at times.

If you sit and do meditation and the asthma causes you to have a hard time, there are other ways to practice. First, you can focus on your steps in walking meditation to get peace of mind and feel relaxed also. Second, you can lie down and have total relaxation and feel your stomach going up on the in breath and down on the exhale. Your breath will be light, but your attention can be down on the expansion of your stomach instead of on your breath. Another way to practice is to use your eyes to look at something directly and see it without putting anything else into it. I call this "Eye-Looking Meditation." When you look at a thing, an object or a person, look at who they are without any whispering voice. Don't go into the past or into whether the person is good or bad. Stop it right there and see it as the real object. It can help you to be refreshed and lively because you see everything as it really is.

When we base our activity on these suggestions, we can pour a cup of tea or eat a bowl of rice and enjoy it. That is meditation, too. You can do everything in daily life and apply the practice of mindfulness to that activity, and then you have peace in each moment.

The next question was from a child who asked what the number is that comes after infinity.

The number that comes after infinity is zero. Zero is the biggest number and contains all of the other numbers, including infinity. Zero has everything within it and contains the whole of the cosmos.

The next question was about practicing at the monastery versus practicing in the city where one works, drives, and generally finds the practice more difficult.

The environment of the monastery is easy because everybody here helps us with the practice, including the mountains and the sangha. At home, there is a turbulence about life, the past, domestic duties, and you don't have the same energy without the support of the sangha. That is why it is hard to practice alone on your own at home.

When you come to the monastery, your priority is to practice. At home, everything is a priority, so the practice is not a priority. If the practice is a priority, there is a method you can use that doesn't add an extra activity into your daily life. You can practice while you do any activity, and then you can learn to do any activity with total relaxation and feel comfortable with everything you do.

Like when you wash the dishes, you can practice mindfulness. Don't make mindfulness practice something else you have to add to your schedule. Instead, when you do your everyday activities, like doing the dishes, do the dishes with total enjoyment. That is the practice. A good practitioner practices and has more energy, not less energy. If we feel like we are doing one more thing when practicing mindfulness, we make it double the load and use a lot of energy.

In other words, try to become one with whatever you are doing. Enjoy it. Relax with it. Then you feel more enjoyment by practicing mindfulness and use less energy. For example, do only one thing at a time. Like if you are driving, don't add another project into the driving. Just drive. Even if an earthquake happens when you are driving, don't put anything else into the driving, or the cooking. Only drive. Only cook.

I sincerely wish you will use the practice and find happiness in the practice.

ABOUT THE EDITOR

Karen Hilsberg, Chân Đại Lượng, True Boundless Graciousness, was ordained in 2004 into the Order of Interbeing, the core community of practitioners in the tradition of Thầy Thích Nhất Hạnh. She is a mother, artist, poet, writer, and clinical psychologist who practices mindfulness in Culver City, California where she lives with her two children and two dogs. This is her first book. To order additional copies of this book, please contact the editor at khilsberg@sbcglobal.net or visit www.lulu.com

ABOUT OUR TEACHER

Most Venerable Thích Nhất Hạnh and the Plum Village Sangha have retreat communities in France, the United States and Vietnam. For more information, please visit www.plumvillage.org or contact:

Plum Village
13 Martineau
33580 Dieulivol, France

Deer Park Monastery
2499 Melru Lane
Escondido, California 92026
Tel: (760) 291-1003

Blue Cliff Monastery
3 Mindfulness Road
Pine Bush, New York 12566

For a worldwide directory of sanghas practicing in this tradition, please visit www.iamhome.org